The Fast Growth Method

What The Top 1% of Coaches, Consultants and Service Providers Are Doing To Scale Their Business

Jag Jassel

Copyright © 2019 Jag Jassel

All Rights Reserved

Creator: Jag Jassel

First Edition: Published in Nov 2019

Disclaimer: The advice provided in this book is general advice only. It has been prepared without considering your objectives, financial situation or business needs. Before acting on this advice you should consider the appropriateness of the advice, having regard to your own objectives, financial situation and business needs. To the maximum extent permitted by law, the author and publisher disclaim all responsibility and liability to any person, arising directly or indirectly from any person taking or not acting based on the information in this book.

Dedication

To my mother, thank you for making me the man I am today.

To my wife Prethika and our kids Aanav & Preja, without your support, sacrifice and belief in me, this work would not be possible.

Acknowledgment

A lot of people believe that there is nothing you can do alone, and you always need the support of someone else around you to help you achieve something. Similar is the case with me. I have a lot of people who played a part in assisting me with the completion of this book and with this section I would like to extend my gratitude towards them.

About the Author

Jag is a business strategist, technology evangelist and Australia's most sought-after business educator. He is the Founder and CEO of **Jassel Media** – No. #1 Marketing Agency for Fast Growth. He helps business owners create 7-8 figure businesses. For more information visit his website: www.jagjassel.com

Preface

This book offers novel ideas that have already garnered the attention of the mainstream and have generated revenue worth millions for various clients. Surprising as it may seem, the secret formula that this book puts forward to accelerate the progression of your business, of course, in financial terms, has been tested and applied in more than 35 niche markets.

The result… is nothing but phenomenal!

There is nothing in the world that comes for free. The ideas and techniques presented in this book come at a price too. In order to reap the benefits of the ideas mentioned in this book, you will have to work hard and dedicate hours to see your efforts reach fruition.

Running a business is a challenge through and through. And one of the most difficult tasks is to be able to grow it. There are countless tips and tricks that you can follow and hope for your business to flourish; however, they are not guaranteed to give you success. There are endless challenges in the market that do not allow a business to grow the way you intend.

What this book offers is a guaranteed way to take your business to the next level. So, are you ready for what this book has in store for you? Are you ready to make your business reach new heights?

With the Fast Growth System, you will be able to start, maintain, and grow your business in ways you never imagined.

To Your Success

Jag Jassel

Contents

Dedication i
Acknowledgment ii
About the Author iii
Preface iv

Chapter 1 1
Introduction
Chapter 2 19
View of the World
Chapter 3 29
Perception vs. Reality
Chapter 4 42
Quantum Mind
Chapter 5 53
Alchemy of Success
Chapter 6 63
Momento Homo
Chapter 7 73
What are you becoming?
Chapter 8 81
How To Achieve Your New Character!
Chapter 9 92
Wealth Opportunities
Chapter 10 102
Your Future Identity
Chapter 11 110
The Transition
Chapter 12 128
Experts Journey
Chapter 13 142
Target Market

Chapter 14	154
Transformation	
Chapter 15	170
Sales in Business	
Chapter 16	182
Client Acquisition	
Chapter 17	195
Proof of Concept (PoC)	
Chapter 18	205
Taking Your Business to the Next Level	
Chapter 19	222
Focus and the Millionaire Path	
Chapter 20	236
Bridging the Gap	
Chapter 21	248
How to Become an Authority to Your Niche Market	
Chapter 22	262
Irresistible Product	
Chapter 23	273
Present to Influence	
Chapter 24	281
Traffic, Leads & Conversion	
Chapter 25	291
The Fast Growth System	

"Elevate yourself so high that even God, before issuing every decree of destiny, should ask you: Tell me, what is your intent?" -

Muhammad Iqbal

World View

Chapter 1
Introduction

"You have to see failure as the beginning and the middle, but never entertain it as an end."

- Jessica Herrin

Dear Friend,

Purchasing this book may turn out to be the smartest decision you have ever made. This book will totally deliver the promise I made in my Ad copy. You are about to learn tried and tested formula to grow your business *FAST*

The ideas mentioned in the book have already generated millions of dollars in revenue for many of our clients. At the time of writing this book, we have applied this secret formula in 35+ niche markets.

Before you begin, I would like to let you know that it will take hard work and dedication from you.

Running a business is not easy, and one of the most difficult tasks is to be able to grow it. There are many tips and tricks you can follow and hope for success; however, they are not guaranteed to give you success. There are numerous different challenges in the market, and

I'm sure you must have attended some programs or have read books to look for ways to grow your business. You must have also practiced those techniques. However, most of the time, when you return home after attending all those events, nothing really happens. You end up doing nothing. You end up realizing you haven't taken any steps or any actions and are still standing where you started.

I grew up in India and was raised by a single mother. In 1998, I came to Australia as a student. While I was studying in Melbourne and pursuing my Masters, I worked at 7/11, factories, drove taxies and did door knocking jobs, etc. Along with all that, I have also established a lot of startups, and after year or two, I would catch myself setting up a startup. During that phase, I lost quite a lot of money as well. I have learned a lot through my experience, the workshops I attended, the books I read, startups I built, and clients I served, and I am more than willing to share that information with the world.

But what I'm going to be sharing with you is very different. With this book, I plan on giving a complete blueprint of the Fast Growth System. This book will help you start, maintain, and grow your business as well as your life. So, consider yourself lucky, because you would have gone out and paid a lot of money to coaches, training centers and universities to understand these concepts. However, I am giving out all of this information in one book for you to benefit from it.

So what is my goal behind this book? Basically, I've got two goals for this. Firstly, I want you to achieve the paradigm shift of your thoughts and beliefs. While you are reading the book, you may have those *"Aha!"* moments and may even have thoughts like, *"Why the hell did I not think of that?"* or things like, *"Holy Sh*t! I never thought of that."*

What I personally want for you is to achieve that paradigm shift and come to the point where you ask yourself why you didn't think of that in the first place. This is what I am looking for because when a change takes place, you start to see and think differently, and that is where life starts to change. Secondly, I want to provide you with a step-by-step plan for Fast Growth. A system which we have been using for the last few years in our business, the same system that hundreds of our clients applied in their businesses as well.

I am looking to help you reach that paradigm shift and make that change in the way you view the world. My biggest belief in the business is that if you want to grow the business, you, as a business owner, must grow yourself first.

We don't have business problems; we have people problems that get reflected in the business.

Now, what we do as a company is that we help people implement those strategies. I understand that not everyone can afford us. Hence, this book is an introduction to our system and strategies that will help you to take your business to that level, where you will be able to afford our product and services. I have learned this system through experience, and it has helped our business grow vastly. I remember about four years ago when we started our first company.

I helped it grow from scratch and successfully exited the business within 12 months. That was our first biggest success. Our second successful milestone was when we started Jassel Media in early 2017, and within 10 months, we were able to take this business to high six-figure revenue.

Numerous people have gone through our live training programs in the last few years. Some of them started from zero and managed to scale their business to high six-figures in just a few months. Few managed to cross the 7-figure mark in just 12 months. Here are some of the messages we have received from our clients.

> Hey Man!! Just wanted to send you this message and let you know what's been happening in my life. I don't know if you recall that we spoke 4 weeks ago. Your 1hr call made so much impact in my life that I started to believe I can do anything... Guess what I did? I resigned from my job and posted on my Facebook wall that I have resigned and now looking for clients. If anyone suffering from depression or anxiety, reach out!
>
> 3 paid clients in the first week.. Lol.. unbelievable! Thank you for giving me the belief
>
> Thank you 🙏
>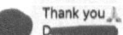

THE FAST GROWTH METHOD

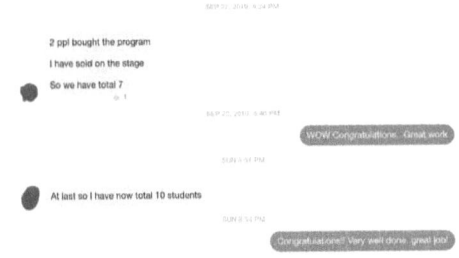

2 ppl bought the program
I have sold on the stage
So we have total 7

WOW Congratulations. Great work

At last so I have now total 10 students

Congratulations!! Very well done, great job!

Phone: +01421004024

Jag. I have now got 10 customers in one week. First time ever. Only one is in Newport. Werribee has gone nuts. Two leads still alive. Both Werribee leads.

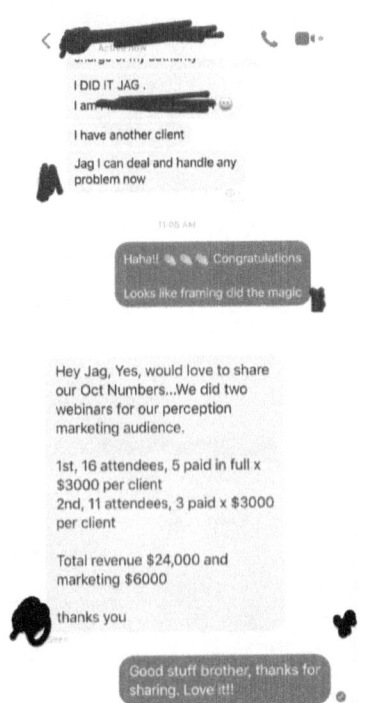

I DID IT JAG.
I am
I have another client
Jag I can deal and handle any problem now

Haha!! 🙌 🙌 🙌 Congratulations
Looks like framing did the magic

Hey Jag, Yes, would love to share our Oct Numbers...We did two webinars for our perception marketing audience.

1st, 16 attendees, 5 paid in full x $3000 per client
2nd, 11 attendees, 3 paid x $3000 per client

Total revenue $24,000 and marketing $6000

thanks you

Good stuff brother, thanks for sharing. Love it!!

JAG JASSEL

> iMessage
> Today 3:34 pm
>
> Hehe, it's ▓▓▓ BTW 3 more clients in last 4 days.

> You are killing it 😄 👍👍👍
> Delivered

> Hey @Jag!
> We had 6 new clients @ $1300 each 🙂

> Yayyyy!! Great results! Congratulations guys

> Today 9:12 pm
>
> Hey Jag!
>
> Just to let you know $7.5 in the bank this month from coaching clients! :)
>
> It took time to put everything in place! I trusted (and put in the work) the process, now getting the results!
>
> My vision of starting my family is now becoming a reality! :)
>
> Thank you so much.

> Wow! Love it... That's so great! Family sounds great. You gonna get busy for sure. Thanks for sharing
> Delivered

> 8:50 AM
>
> Hey Jag... 18k this month and 1300 on advertising ▓▓▓▓▓▓
> 👍 1

> 10:43 AM
>
> Good stuff brother!!

> Jag, guess what? we did our best month ever! $52K in sales... Money in the bank. Thanks mate, couldn't have done it without you
>
> Thank you

>> Congratulations to you and team Steve! Love it
>> Delivered

Let's look at the back-end of the business and how I was able to grow businesses so easily. I was a person who failed badly at startups and was unable to succeed for many years of my life. I spent many years of my life struggling to make a startup successful. Then, one day, a shift took place in my life. I will be sharing that story with you in this book.

However, this is to inform you that the shift I experienced was not through some sort of steps. It was not that somebody gave me some *"how-to"* steps, and I followed them and ended up succeeding. No! That was not the case at all. The shift was about me completely changing my mindset and the way I saw the world. I call it perception, or the view of the world. The moment you change your view of the world, things automatically start to change. That is what happened to me, personally. In these pages to come, I have tried to tell the story of my stupid mistakes and precisely what I did that lifted me out of those blunders. I hope you will overlook and forgive me for using the personal pronoun *"I."* If there is anything in this book that sounds as though I'm bragging about myself, I didn't intend in that way. Whatever bragging I have done was meant for what these ideas did for me and what they will do for anyone who will apply them.

Here, I have attempted to write the kind of book that I tried to find when I first started my first business. Nevertheless, one important point I want to raise before we get started with this book is that I am not good at everything. Some of you may be the best accountants, while I am a person who sucks at accounting. Some of you may be great coaches and are really good at coaching because you have gone through the required training. Some of you, on the other hand, maybe amazing real estate agents, or some of you could be the ideal parents.

I do not want to claim that I am good at everything. However, one thing I am really proud of is that I am great at growing businesses in a short period of time. If someone is looking for ways to grow their business *FAST*, then I am certainly the guy for the job. This is because I have done it quite a lot of times and helped hundreds of other people just like you.

The major reason for my success is that I understand human psychology. Thanks to my understanding of human psychology and the ability to apply the principles that lead to success, growing business becomes extremely simple after that. I understand the reasons that make a human move from point A to B, and that is what helps me a lot in almost anything I do. Whether it is a business or something pertaining to my personal life, or even if it means me conversing with someone one-on-one, human psychology makes me understand why & how the other person makes the decisions the way he or she does. Human psychology is pretty simple; if you put culture away, every human is the same underneath. We all have the same needs, we all have the same wants, and we all have the same desires. Once you understand humans, growing your business becomes so much easier.

Things are much better now, and I can do whatever I want to do, and through this, I have been able to help a lot of people. However, things were not like this initially. I remember the time when my school English teacher said to me, *"Jag, you can't speak English."* Even though she said that to me once, yet it replayed in my mind for several years till the age of 35. Whenever anything would not go in my favor, I would blame it on my English-speaking skills. There were many times when I stopped myself all because of my lack of English.

Many years ago, I was working as an enterprise architect for big companies such as IBM and ORACLE, and one of the good things working for those companies as a contractor was that I was being paid a good amount of money. I was paid enough that I did not have to think twice about buying something. Despite being able to get everything, I had that itch in me to start a business of my own. Due to that itch, I kept struggling a lot, and I failed quite a lot of times. It was a dark time of my life where nothing was working, and no success was coming my way. No matter what I tried, nothing seemed to work. I had a good job, yet I was doing a lot of side hustles. I have established a lot of startups, such as a car sales platform, a job search platform, and I have even set up classified-type of websites, I have provided training in IT, as well as I have provided a lot of consulting services. Despite the various types of work, nothing seemed to work for me. I became really frustrated with life!

My journey started in 2015 when I met Tony Robbins for the first time at his event called UPW in Sydney. After that, I met a lot of people in person and became a part of their masterminds. Tony Robbins, Brendon Burchard, Russell Brunson, Napoleon Hill, and Ray Dalio are some intellectuals from whom I learned a lot from. I read more than 700+ books in the last few years.

Books had a significant difference in my life, and one particular topic I focused on was Human Psychology. I have read most of the books on the planet related to Human Psychology, how does it work, and how do we work as humans. Also, one other thing, which helped me tremendously in the last few years, was meditation. I have taken numerous meditation trainings, and I have spent a lot of time with the Monks to understand our mind-body connection.

I recently came back after I was away for 10 days on training for meditation, where I was away from gadgets and everything electronic. I have learned a lot from that, and that is what I will be teaching you in the first part of my book.

A major shift in my life took place after I met those influencers and good people in the world. They taught me some things that brought a shift to my life. My life turned upside down. I couldn't believe it myself, but it happened.

What changed my life?

Things that changed my life started with my **beliefs**.

Firstly, I am a big believer in energy. I truly believe If people are coming together, they are bringing their energy. If we operate at higher energy vibration, good things happen to us. If we operate at low energy vibration, the so-called bad things happen. So for the sake of maintaining high vibration to the entire reader community of this book, I would like to recommend that you take full responsibility of what type of energy you are bringing to this book reading community.

It is imperative that you must bring positive energy or higher vibration energy into the group. Another important point I want to mention is, park your old learning on the side while you are reading this book. Some of the things I am going to share in this book won't make sense initially, but I just want you to be open to trying new things and accepting them with a new belief. I just want you to use one word when you don't believe it might be true for you…*"Interesting"*…Just say, *"Interesting, I have never thought that way before!"*

Have you ever wondered how others' belief systems may be impacting you? You may know some people who have been working for a while and who have developed their own view of the world. They may say something like, *"It is just a startup, and you are never going to make money in the first two years of the business"* or *"this is very common, you are never going to make a profit in the first 6 months."* Let me tell you that this is all rubbish stuff, and they are just trying to implement their belief onto you. Your job is not to get hung on this because you can make money as fast as tomorrow. I am just going to put this out there that there will be a lot of things that will not make sense to you, and that is because they are not supposed to make sense. The thoughts you have developed in the past, I am working to change those thoughts for a better future.

Secondly, take action. Without action, all this information has no meaning. It is simple; if you do not take the necessary action and apply this training in your life, then nothing will help you grow your business. So if there is anything you want to do, please take action because if you don't, nothing will change. As I said, we are all bringing positive energy. Therefore, you do not want to be one of those people who pulls others down.

Also, join our online community Facebook group called Fast Growth Tribe. Here's the link:

https://www.facebook.com/groups/fastgrowthtribe

Why is it hard to be successful?

Let us talk more in-depth about understanding why most people are unable to succeed. There is dark energy that holds them back. Let me explain this; there are two kinds of people out there. One of them is those who do not know much and do not have enough knowledge, yet they are successful. On the contrary, there are those people who know a lot of things and have vast knowledge about everything, yet they are not successful in life. Why?

Everyone knows what they need to do, but they just don't do it. Why? Why do they hope and dream for the things but never seem to be able to achieve them? Why do human beings hope, pray, and dream for things they have never been able to achieve? Why do they take few positive steps towards their dreams and goals and then sabotage themselves? Why do humans do that?

The answer is because they have this feeling that something is holding them back or they are not good enough. Sometimes there is a feeling that something out there is holding me back. Like for example, you are trying to move forward, yet you take two steps backward. The question is, what is this thing I am referring to as *dark energy* that seems to be against you and making you suffer? What is holding you back, and what is the reason you can't achieve your goal?

I was a big believer of steps. Earlier in my career, I worked for big corporations. Therefore I relied on steps/processes/systems a lot. I would always look for steps in order to complete a task and achieve the goal. So, what I used to do was whenever I learned something, I would create proper steps / system for it (e.g., How to do ____ using the three-step system). I would then guide people by showing them the right steps. Despite showing them the right steps, some never took any action. This thing always intrigued me as to why people were NOT taking action in achieving their goals, even though I had given them all the steps. The answer I found was that they didn't believe that they could be successful. They just didn't believe that by taking action on those steps, they would achieve their desired results; hence, no action!

Everybody has their own view of the world. Everybody sees things differently, and that is called **Perception**. Everybody has got their own perception. Let's look at an example of some blind men. These blind men are taken to an elephant and are asked to describe what they feel. Each blind person describes the elephant based on what they touched. For example, if one would touch its tail, he would describe it as a snake. The other blind person touched the body of the elephant and described it as a rough wall. What I mean to say is, we all have our own view of things. Our view is based on the values, the time, and the culture we are born in. Therefore, each of us has developed this perception, which is different from the other. In the business world, when we believe in a certain way, we assume that everybody out there sees things the same way as us. This is a very common mistake. If I am excited about something, I would expect others to feel the same. What we fail to understand is that all human beings have their own perceptions of everything.

Once you understand this fact and believe it, it becomes much easier to grow your business. During my journey, one thing I have observed is that successful people think and see things differently as compared to 99% of the world. They see things, perceive things, and they believe in things very differently.

I would like to share a story of the time when I was in Singapore, and I stayed a few days with a multi-millionaire, and out of respect, I called him Uncle. He was not related to me, but I knew him through a very close friend of mine. He was one of the richest men in the world who owned many hotels in Singapore. I would like to share a funny story that this one time when I walked into his house after he picked me up from the airport. I saw that he had so many statues outside his house, which had a market value of $200,000 each. All I could think of was that it would take me around 10 years or more to have all of that.

One night, when we finished dinner and were sitting on his dining table and watching TV, suddenly something came up on the news. I noticed my uncle got up, and he left the table. I was surprised yet determined to ask him what happened. So the next day at the breakfast table, I asked him why he left the table. He replied, *"Jag, I don't watch the news. I avoid seeing anything negative out there. I want to make sure that my mind is not filled with negativity."*

I did not understand it at first, and initially, my thoughts were, *"What a selfish guy."* However, after he explained that watching the news on TV generated negative thoughts within him and made him depressed, it didn't benefit anyone. He runs many charities and directly helps those in need. I know by now that some of you might be thinking you need to watch the news so that you know what's happening in the world. My question to that would be, *why?* Why do you need to know everything? If there is anything urgent, believe me, someone will notify you, so you don't have to fill your mind with all this useless information.

THE FAST GROWTH METHOD

Coming to this point, here is a question you need to answer. Do you think you have a chance to be successful in your life? Do you feel that there is even a tiny chance for you to be successful and wealthy? Let me give you the answer. There is no chance at all. There is dark energy stopping you, and it is to be blamed for everything. It is the dark energy that is holding you back and stopping you from being successful and wealthy. Now the question is, what is that dark energy?

*This dark energy is YOU. YOU are the only one stopping yourself from taking your life and your business to the next level. It is not your skills, your past, your location, your government, your age, your tech skills, your mom and dad, your face, your body, or anything else; it is just **YOU**.*

It is easy to blame someone or something else. The moment you blame something/someone else, you lose forever. When you blame something/someone else, you are giving them the power to take control of your life, and that is why things do not go the way you want them to go. Hence, in life, there is only one person to blame for your losses, and that person is **YOU**.

You have to take responsibility for everything you do, either good or bad. Take control of your ship. This is your ship, and you are the sailor of it. You need to be responsible and drive your own life because no one else will do that for you. To move forward and grow in life, you have to leave your old identity behind. In order to become a successful person, you need to *become a person who deserves success*.

You have to become a better version of yourself. If you are ready to take the FULL responsibility of your life and business going forward, then you are ready for the next chapter! Always remember rule no. 1 – take FULL responsibility for your life and your business.

Chapter 2
View of the World

"Change the way you look at things and the things you look at change."

— *Wayne W. Dyer*

In the previous chapter, I have talked about having a perception. Everyone has a perception of his/her own. In this regard, I quoted an example in the previous chapter about blind people and an elephant. As each blind person touches the elephant, he/she describes it as per his/her own perception. Another example could be of two people who witness an accident at the same time, yet each of them describes it differently. This is because everyone has their own perception, which is known as the *World View*.

Everyone has their own world view. My main goal of this book is to create a paradigm shift for you so that you can grow your business **FAST**! Also, in order to bring a change, we need to go back to where the initial problem lies. The main problem is how we see the world today. Once you are aware of how you see the world, it becomes easier to take it to the next level and make the necessary changes.

Success in life is 80% psychology and 20% mechanics – Tony Robbins. When I came across this quote, it took me a while to grasp the quote. I was not sure of what he actually meant by 80% psychology. I spent some time trying to understand this concept of psychology. I have asked the same question in my events as well. What did he mean by 80% psychology? Many people responded back with responses like positive attitude, your habits, mindset etc.

What I understood was that **80% is actually your own view of the world**. It is about how you see things, and view the world and portray your understanding of the world. It includes factors like how you deal with people, how you run your business, what you believe in, how you talk to people, and how you respond etc. All of these add up to form 80% of psychology. Whatever it may be, it is the ultimate truth for you. It is your view of the world.

As we all see the world differently and have our own view of the world, therefore that is where the problem originates from. There are a number of problems that influence us because of our perception. When we look at the world, we forget that each individual in this world has their own perception and their own way of viewing the world. That's when we have this mindset that we are right, and the other person is wrong. When you understand this concept of world view, you begin to accept the view of other people.

You accept that they have their own opinions and perceptions.

Let's look at *Classical Physics and Quantum Physics*. Classical physics refers to theories of physics that predate modern, more complete, or more widely applicable theories. This is the type of physics that has been taught in books with all those theories and laws. Then there is quantum physics. This type of physics completely changes the way we see things. It is a completely different study as compared to classical physics. People who support quantum physics are totally against the ones who support classical physics. They have their own ways of looking at things.

Victim Identity

It is where every person plays the victim in his story. They label themselves as the victim. This is because they feel that it is their identity, and they belong in that position, and when someone says something about their identity, they feel that they are being attacked. Hence, this chapter is mostly going to cover *identity* as a topic. For someone to build an identity, they have to let go of the past and move forward. To reach the next level in life, one has to move out of the unsettling phase of life, and unless that happens, you are stuck in that phase.

How to always stay positive?

A lot of people have questioned me as to how can I remain so positive, and how can I look for solutions and not focus on the problem? My answer to them has always been the same, *"my new view of the world."* I see the world differently due to my view of the world. I had to make some changes within myself in order to come out of the old view and create a new view of the world. This is what I want to give to you in the form of this book. Hopefully, after reading this book, you will be one of those people in your group that will see everything as an opportunity and not as a problem.

It is a known fact that the surprises that we don't like come to us as problems, whereas the surprises that we have been waiting for are loved a lot by us. At the end of the day, we all wish to be limitless and not be blocked by any obstacle that comes in our way. However, we need to be bold enough to go out there and do the stuff that we love so much, irrespective of the hindrances that may come our way. Through this book, I want you to become that limitless person that each of you thinks and dreams of. Some examples of being limitless include actions that we do unconsciously or sometimes even consciously. For example, some people have a perception that there are not many ideas left in the world to pursue. Therefore, they lack the motivation in pursuing their dreams. Another example is when one thinks they are unable to make more money because they are either too young, too old, too dark, or too white.

There are also times when people have this perception that in order to be spiritual, you have to be poor. It is a misconception that people are unable to make money because they are not of a particular race or ethnicity. Another major example of being bound by limitations is when one's significant other does not support them.

I had a similar limitation when my teacher told me that I couldn't speak English. I replayed that sentence in my head repeatedly to the limit that I believed that I couldn't speak English, and that is why I cannot move forward. Now I want you to ask yourself, what is that reason that makes you limit yourself? What is that one thing that you have told yourself due to which you are reluctant to move forward? If you are someone who makes any of the reasons that I have mentioned earlier, then you need to understand that you need to change the way you see the world. It is very easy to point out flaws in others. However, it is not an easy task to fix what is wrong within ourselves. Like, how do you see the world? That is where the problem arises. Unless you fix yourself internally, you cannot see the world in full transparency. Let me state a personal story about when I used to work at a café as a dishwasher. I remember this girl who was working with me, she came and said to me that I smelled really bad. She asked me if I had a shower.

I'm sure she had good intentions, and she said it to me in a very good tone with a smile on her face. Even though she didn't criticize me, her words kept revolving around my head to the point I started feeling bad about it. I didn't come to work for a week, and eventually, I left that job. This is how I was. This is how I viewed the world. Everything was a personal attack on my identity.

Your business and how to grow it?

As you are growing, you will have the chance and the opportunity to be working with a number of different people, such as employees, clients, spouses, friends, colleagues, etc. Therefore, *your growth depends on the number of tough conversations that you will be having with these people.* You will have to learn how to make these tough conversations because, without them, you will be unable to grow yourself and broaden your view of the world.

In the past, I was not a person who loved tough conversations. I had a habit of running away from these conversations. I never stood up for myself, and instead, I ran away from them. This was not the case between me and my colleagues only, but even with my wife, relatives, friends and my mother; whenever we were supposed to have a tough conversation I would just run away because I did not want to face reality.

That is when I realized that the more I avoided those conversations, the more conflicts I faced. I realized that I had to face those conflicts, and that was when I started growing as a person, which helped me grow my business ultimately. For example, when you work out in the gym, your muscle becomes accustomed to the workout, and eventually, it starts gaining shape physically. In the same way, you need to face your conflicts and tough conversations in order to grow yourself.

The Law of Nature states that everything evolves. In the same way, we human beings have evolved too. Life is not static, and everything is moving. Nothing is ever constant.

Why is it that we know what we have to do, yet we do not take that step? As I mentioned earlier, everything in this world is meant to grow. Humans, plants, businesses, everything is supposed to grow. However, the problem is the attachment with *Identity,* or you can call it Identity Crisis.

Let's take an example of someone who is easily annoyed. If you know someone around you who is easily annoyed by even slight inconvenience, then that person has a strong attachment to their identity.

If you want to be a writer, you have to think of yourself of being a writer and then becoming that person. Apparently, this is where people lack. They do not see themselves as the person they picture themselves. This is the gap that needs to be filled. In order to become someone who you want to be, you need to get out of your comfort zone. People have this thought that self is an illusion, and they see themselves as a static person. Since they see themselves as a static person, their life becomes static.

You need to see yourself evolving. You need to measure yourself that today you are here, and you need to be there. That is when you succeed in life. We, humans, are paralyzed by the thoughts of self. People are not prepared to change, and that is where they make a mistake. They cannot do the things they want to without making the necessary change. You have the power to create your own world view.

New View of the World

We have analyzed the problem that is viewing the world as static and not making a change to move along with the world. So, the first thing you should do in order to become something is that you need to remove the static thought and leave the old identity behind. I did not attend universities and gained degrees to be where I am today. In fact, my degrees made me a better employee. To become a successful business owner, I had to leave behind my old employee world and create a new world view for myself. To become somebody else, I had to change my identity and remove my static self.

If you look at yourself today, you are certainly NOT where you want to be. However, you can bring the necessary changes and become everything you want to be today by shifting your identity. Everyone today is going somewhere and taking their lives to the next level. So now the question is, what do you plan on becoming? Where are you going in life? For me, I am becoming a fast growth authority who is helping business owners scale their business ***FAST***. Therefore, you need to start and become the person that you want to be.

Why Success is Hard?

As I mentioned earlier, we are all meant to grow. However, the sad reality is that despite being aware of the hindrances and their goal, people are still unwilling to bring the required changes in themselves. They are stuck in their current reality. They want to achieve their goals but not willing to let go who they are. They must let go of the current identity, and then only they can achieve their desired future.

People blame the environment for their failures. They blame their environment for not succeeding in life. The environment includes friends, family, living conditions, government, etc. They are attached to their identity, and that is why gaining success becomes almost impossible for them. The moment they let go of their identity, that is when things will start to change.

Chapter 3
Perception vs. Reality

"Perception is more important than reality. If someone perceives something to be true, it is more important than if it is in fact true."

*— **Ivanka Trump***

In this chapter, I will discuss something that I enjoy talking about. I talk about this in my conferences, events, and almost everywhere. That is: *Perception vs. Reality*

*"When you grow up, you tend to get told the world is the way it is, and life is just to live your life inside the world. Try not to bash into the walls too much. Try to have a nice family, have fun, save a little money. That's a very limited life. Life can be much broader once you discover one simple fact: Everything around you that you call life was **made up** by people that were no smarter than you and you can change it, you can influence it, and you can build your own things that other people can use. Once you learn that, you'll never be the same again."*- Steve Jobs

Out of the many quotes, this is one of the quotes that had a profound effect on my life. When I came across this, it changed the entire landscape of my understanding of human beings. Not only that, but it also changed my view of the world. As the quote states that everything around us is *made up* by people just like you and me. It is not created by any super humans; all of them are simple people just like us. Once we understand this simple rule, it becomes easy to change or challenge these rules. We perceive that all of this is done by people who have studied at universities, earned their PhDs and the like.

We start making assumptions that in order for you to change any of these rules, you must have certain qualifications or experience etc. However, if you look at it, all of this is not done by people who are better than you or are smarter than you. Its just people like you who did it.

Let the Law of Nature do the Work

As I have mentioned earlier in the previous chapters that everything is meant to grow. You cannot force things to happen. Everything eventually works out the way it is supposed to.

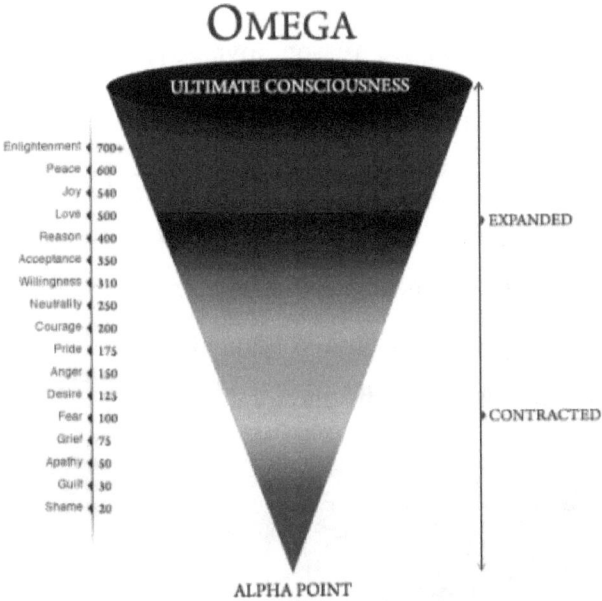

Figure 1: Chart of Consciousness

The above chart was extracted from a book called Power vs. Force. If you take a look at this chart, you will see the values of energy on the left-hand side. We always refer to people having low energies or high energies. Those energies are denoted with the numbers in the figure. This chart defines that everybody is on a different energy level depending on the *state of mind* and the *emotion* that they are in.

Looking at the chart, if you have emotions like shame, guilt, apathy, grief, etc. then you have low vibrations. People who experience such emotions for a long period of time tend to operate in low-level energy. People who experience emotions such as willingness, acceptance, reason, love, joy, etc.

They operate at very high frequencies in life. When people operate in this energy, things tend to attract them. On the contrary, people who work at very low energies tend to force things to happen. If you are one of those people who struggle and force things to happen, then you may have a faint idea that things become really hard, and that is where the energy does not align.

Level	Log	Emotion	Life View
Enlightenment	700 – 1000	Ineffable	Is
Peace	600	Bliss	Perfect
Joy	540	Serenity	Complete
Love	500	Reverence	Benign
Reason	400	Understanding	Meaningful
Acceptance	350	Forgiveness	Harmonious
Willingness	310	Optimism	Hopeful
Neutrality	250	Trust	Satisfactory
Courage	200	Affirmation	Feasible
Pride	175	Scorn	Demanding
Anger	150	Hate	Antagonistic
Desire	125	Craving	Disappointing
Fear	100	Anxiety	Frightening
Grief	75	Regret	Tragic
Apathy	50	Despair	Hopeless
Guilt	30	Blame	Evil
Shame	20	Humiliation	Miserable

In the chart above, the left-hand side talks about the levels of energy, then comes the log, which is the value of the energy mentioned. The third column describes the emotion that you are feeling at that time, and the fourth column describes the life view. Life view is related to the world's view that I have described in the previous chapter.

Let's pick the energy of Pride. At that time, your life's view is demanding, and you are demanding everything to happen. Even in the energy of courage, you are experiencing affirmations. Emotionally your mind says, *"I want to make things happen,"* and these are the affirmations that you are making to yourself. That is when your life's view becomes feasible.

Lastly, if you look at enlightenment, the life-view for an enlightened person is nothing but *"is."* Nothing more and nothing less, it is just *"is."* My intention is to make you reach a higher level of energy and operate in it. When you enter the high level of energy, you enter into that space where things automatically happen for you instead of you forcing things to happen. With the high level of energy, your emotional state changes, and with the change of emotional state, you will eventually change your life view. When you change your level of emotion, things will happen the way the law of nature works.

What is Reality?

Reality is defined differently in different contexts. I will define reality based on different religions. According to Buddha, the reality is *"yatha-bhuta."* This means *"as it is."* According to Hinduism, under the function of Brahman, reality is the eternal truth and bliss, which does not change. As per the Bible, reality is something that is supreme and final.

To conclude the above-mentioned, it implies that reality comprises of things the way they are. There is nothing made up in it; it is exactly how things are.

Types of Reality
- Universal Reality – Rules of the Universe (The Law of Nature)
- Agreed Reality – Our planet agreed on some standard rules
- Perceived Reality – Everything remaining is Perceived Reality.

Universal Reality

Universal reality is the law that is not governed by anyone but nature. For example, our Earth is hanging in the Universe, the stars are hanging in the Universe, and everything is revolving around the sun. If you plant a tree today, that tree is meant to grow. That is a universal rule. Universal reality has been around before man made anything else.

When humans came to existence on this planet, there used to be war and fights. There was a time when humans were always at war. If they had a son, he would also grow up to fight in the war. Therefore, people grew sensible and created agreed realities to stop the continuous war.

Agreed Reality

Agreed reality is also known as a set of rules for humans to live on this planet. Greeks and Romans were the ones who created those rules really well. Before these rules were created, people were unaware of how to carry out activities. These rules gave people the direction of right and wrong. For example, the months of the year have a specific name; these are agreed reality. However, the Chinese did not agree on it, so they created their own calendar.

Perceived Reality

Perceived reality is the reality, which is everything else other than Agreed Reality and Universal Reality. How certain communities or countries believe in a certain way. For them, it is very real. For Example, some communities can eat beef, but others are frowned upon.

How do Humans See the World?

This is a study that was conducted by a Harvard Professor between the years 1950-1960. This study is called the ladder experience. In this study, they talked more about the experiences of human beings. In a nutshell, it talked about how human beings see the world. Even though this study was conducted decades ago; however, it is still being talked about after all these years.

This Professor created a Ladder Rung Experience Rule. This rule explains that as human beings, we pick up raw data through observations and experiences. As you pick up raw data, you filter that data through your experiences, beliefs, and values.

After that, you create meaning out of the understanding of that data. Once you have your meanings created, you then create assumptions based on them. Then you go ahead and create a conclusion out of it, and your emotions are attached to it. After which you have a solid belief in the conclusion. And that is when you take action based on that belief that you have. Let's take a look at an example. Let's say you are trying to park a car. You are driving past the parking lot, and you see an empty space. However, as you are observing things and trying to park, another car comes in and parks into your spot. You are left standing and without a parking spot. As you were observing things, you noted that this other car is now parked in your spot. Now your mind filters the situation. You think of how rude that person is and how ill-mannered he is.

You also think about whether or not this person has the ethics to behave in public. After that, you create a meaning to the filters which you have created. You create whether this was a bad or a good incident. When you perceive a meaning that what this person did is bad, you start creating assumptions. You assume that this person was not given proper education, which is why he did what he did. This is how you create a conclusion based on your assumption. Then you create your belief based on that conclusion. Lastly, you act on the entire situation based on your belief.

You pull your windows down and start screaming at that person. This person gets out of the car, apologizes, explains that his wife is pregnant, and he needs to get her to the emergency, which is why he needed the parking really urgently. This is when your reality crashes and your action changes since you assumed something based on the filters that you created. Therefore, everything changed after you learned about reality.

Perception

Perception is basically how you make of what you experience. It is your version of reality and not what everyone else thinks it is.

Perception is not reality; however, everyone thinks it is. You might wonder why that is the case. The reason is that everyone goes through this ladder of experience. Everyone is experiencing life based on this ladder, and that is why it is a perception and not a reality.

What Creates Perception?

In the last many decades, science has defined everything. Due to these definitions given by science, things have been separated. The moment that a part of an object is defined, that part is then separated from the entire object. Even in real life, if things are not defined, people do not see them because of the conscious mind only able to see the things that have been defined. So how do we create perception?

When you define something, you create an assumption about that particular thing. When you have an assumption, there are 5 to 6 ideas that come to your mind. However, when the assumptions keep re-occurring, we create a belief about it. And when the belief is created, our thoughts become aligned with our beliefs. These thoughts of ours then create reality.

Allow me to elaborate with the help of an example. A kid always sees his parents fight. And whenever they fight, they always mention the word *"money."* Now, this boy is not aware of what money is. Therefore, he ignores it and goes back to doing what he was doing. However, when another fight occurs, he hears the same word. Now, whenever his parents argue, he hears the same word. This boy now builds the perception that whenever money is involved, there is always going to be a fight. Therefore, he tries his best to avoid money and avoid any fights in his life. This is why he is left behind and is not able to earn and be successful. In order for him to be successful and for him to move forward in life, he needs to change his perception, and his reality will eventually change. Most of the times these beliefs are so ingrained that the conscious mind is not even aware of it.

In the context of business, when you are in the market, the market sets a definition for you. The market defines you for who you are and what you do. As soon as you are defined, you are separated from the rest of the market. For example, if you are a consultant, you are defined by your work. That is what separates you from the rest of the consultants. The human mind is not aware of the difference between reality and imagination. The mind gets information through the five senses; however, the mind also receives information through our imagination. The mind is unable to differentiate, which is real and which is just an imagination. Therefore, there is a famous quote that says, *"You create your reality twice."* You create it once in your imagination and the second in reality.

Modes of Awareness
- Perception – Like explained extensively in the chapter, perception is what you have perceived. It has nothing to do with reality; it is simply a perception of the mind.
- Intuition – The only way to tap into intuition is to stop thinking. The most effective way of getting into the gut space is to stop thinking and start doing. People who believe that they have a gut feeling; they do not rely 100% on their brains. Rather they simply believe in their gut feel and go with the flow.

The Big Problem
Here's the big problem I am keep seeing after working with hundreds of clients.
- We always try to understand everything. We need to stop finding the meaning of everything and simply let things be as they are.
- To understand things, we begin to define everything. That is where we separate things from each other.

- When we define things, we become bias toward things that are attractive to us.
- The answer to the big problem is that we do not need to understand everything. That moment is called Innocence. We need to bring innocence in us and let things be as they are.

Once you understand these concepts, it is important for you to apply them in the business world. The reason is, it is very easy to change the perception of anything. That is why I always say that perception is a reality. When we change our perception, we are changing our reality.

Chapter 4
Quantum Mind

"Consciousness ... is the phenomenon whereby the universe's very existence is made known"

- Roger Penrose

As I have mentioned earlier that there is a huge debate going on in the science world about classical physics and quantum physics. When Einstein wrote his paper on general theory of relativity, he discussed a lot of stuff about classic physics. However, there were some things that he just wasn't able to answer. Some things were a complete mystery to him and he called them the "greatest blunder".

Moving on, this chapter will discuss Quantum Mind. What is the quantum mind, and what does it have to do with business and personal growth? This book is all about fast growth, and we all want to grow and take our lives and businesses to the next level. I truly believe that moving away from monkey mind to quantum mind is the quickest and fastest way!

We will start off with Sir Roger Penrose, who talked about *"The Quantum Nature of Consciousness"* in his book *"The Emperor's*

New Mind." Sir Roger Penrose is a mathematician and is now also a physicist. I have stated in the previous chapter that when you observe things, you are actually describing things. And when you want to define something or understand something, you have to create a separation. This is where the Computational Mind (or monkey mind) comes from. The computational mind is responsible for solving and calculating stuff. Our mind works like a computer and solves our problems for us.

The other mind that Sir Roger Penrose refers to is the Unconscious Activities that are activated by the unconscious mind. These activities are not governed by the computational activities; neither are they monitored by your mind. This means that you are completely unaware when carrying out these activities.

In the previous chapter, we have studied about how perception is different from reality, how we are responsible for everything, the different modes of awareness, and how people see and receive information. You must be wondering as to why we are focusing on thought so much. Well, here is why. If you are looking to have a paradigm shift in your life, the first step in doing so is to change the way you *think*.

Changing your way of thought is not an easy process because you are surrounded by the same people that have the same thought as yours. So, the question is, where do you get your new thinking from?

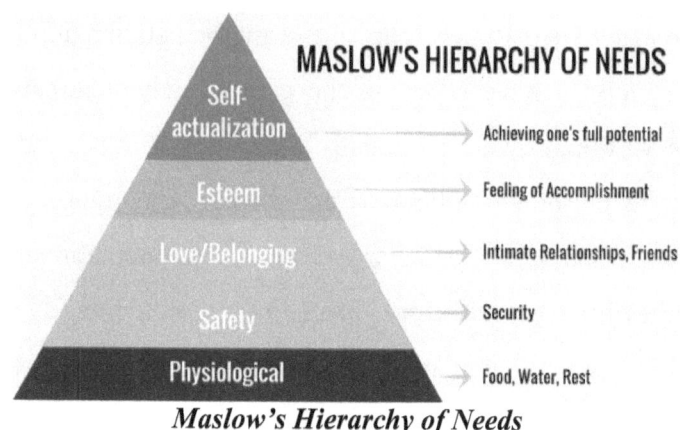

Maslow's Hierarchy of Needs

We are all aware of Maslow's Hierarchy of Needs. We all have the needs which start from physiological needs to safety needs, belongingness, and then to esteem. However, in this chapter, our main focus is going to be Self-Actualization. The question is, how do you develop that if the end goal is to rise to the top? What do you do if your child comes up to you asking to buy something they want and you do not have the money for it? So these are such situations on which we will be focusing on.

People evolve. And as we have talked about it earlier, you are not the same person you were a few years ago. With time, you have changed and developed and have moved forward in life. In order for you to move to the next level, you must think about *who you are becoming*!

There was this one incident that has made a huge impact on me as a person. We were in Fiji a few of years ago, staying at Tony Robbin's resort. I had the privilege of being there for an event. One of the exercises that I did as part of the event was to climb a pole. I had the harness on the back, and I simply had to climb the pole.

There were no side support available, so I had to put my foot over the other to properly balance myself, and when I reached the top, I had to jump a free fall from there. So to accomplish this exercise, I climbed the pole really fast. However, when I reached the top, I pretty much froze. I froze to the extent that I couldn't take a step further. So I stood there for around 3 to 4 minutes, but for me, it felt like a lifetime. When I gathered my courage, I finally made the jump. After a good 8 to 10 minutes, I put my feet on the ground. As I reached the ground, Laz (one of the coaches) came up to me and took me to the side. He said to me one thing that really changed my world view. After asking me some questions about the incident. He said, *"Jag, the way you do one thing, the way you do everything!"* I asked, what do you mean Laz?

He said, *"the way you do one thing, the way you do everything"* Now look back in your life and see, where else you are not taking the next step? You know what need to be done, you have the support and you have people those are cheering for you but you are NOT taking any action.

This was when I realized that I know what need to be done next in my life & business but I am not taking any action.

So, when I got back from Fiji, I knew I needed to get into making videos. Therefore, in the first three months of coming back to Melbourne, I got busy making videos through my phone. I never uploaded that content; I just did it to practice talking in front of the camera.

Who Are You As a Person?

We have talked about this repeatedly, that you are programmed with everything. You may get it from your family, friends, environment, the way you were raised, etc. You have your perception, your culture, and your values from people related to you. You did not make all of this up; instead, somebody else gave it to you. Somebody else helped in making you the person that you are today. However, now is the time that you think about taking over the control and create your own reality.

Have you ever thought why are the rich getting richer, and the middle and lower classes are still static despite getting the right education? Why can some people not afford a cup of coffee while there are people who buy houses in expensive areas on a daily basis? This intrigued me to find out why people are not able to be rich despite their hard work and their dedication.

People have been told that in order to earn more money, they need to climb the ***ladder of University education***. However, as per my observation, Ph.D. holders are earning only about $150,000 to $200,000 a year. This is nothing as compared to rich people. This statement is a complete lie.

80-20 Rule

It is well-known that 80% wealth of a country is owned by 20% of its people. 80% of the earth is water, and 20% of it is land. In the same way, 80% crime in the world is committed by 20% of the people. Also, 80% of the traffic usually happens on 20% of the streets. Out of that 20% streets with traffic, only 20% have more traffic than the other 80%. So, now think of complaining about 80%. There is a thing called the Feedback Loop, and understanding this term will help you to not complain about the 80% going on in this world.

The Feedback Loop

It is also referred to as the Cause & Effect. For example, the more you use the air-conditioner, release more CO_2 in the air. This causes an increase in the weather, which makes you use the air-conditioner even more. The same way, the more money is deposited in the banks, the more they earn interest. The interest increases the amount of money in the bank; therefore, more interest is charged. This is the feedback loop. The feedback loop is a powerful phenomenon.

It is so powerful that it works positively as well as negatively in your life. Anything that you do today turns the feedback loop on. It can be positive or negative. As I said earlier, we live with the same values and thoughts as our family members. If one person starts living under a specific value or thought, eventually the feedback loop starts, and everyone in the family starts living under that thought and value.

Having the thought that you are going to accomplish something and that you will get the job will further generate more positive thoughts. This habit is meant to either make you or break you. This can either make you huge or destroy you.

The entire purpose of this book is to grow your business as well as personal life. My goal is that by the end of this book, your new habits have been generated, and you continue with those habits even after finishing the book. What I am looking for is for you to create a life based on your terms and not on your family or friends.

Warren Buffet

Let's take a look at Warren Buffet's age and net worth.

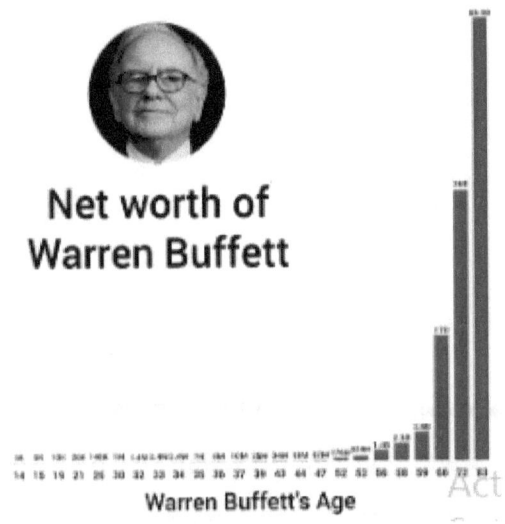

During the beginning years, his net worth was pretty straightforward, until the age of 47. After that, things just took a boost. During his last years, his worth grew to $58.5 billion. The question is, why and how did that happen? Everything started with a thought process. I am going to quote my example in this situation. I came up with the thought that *"I am going to master how to grow a business fast."* This thought then took me to the next level, where I said that *"I am going to be the authority of fast business growth."* This works as a feedback loop. As I start to see results of my clients, I start to think more positive thoughts.

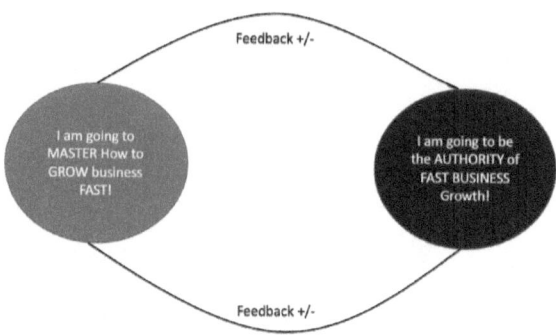

It may seem interesting, but how does it actually work, you may ask? Only when you begin to walk on the path and believe that something is going to happen is when it actually happens.

I've learned a lot of stuff through the way marketing and digital marketing work, such as YouTube videos, for example. What I discovered is that there is always a pattern, and the patterns were interconnected. If there is anybody who is not rich today, there is a pattern behind it. The reason is that everything is interconnected. The thoughts that you have in your mind while making a sales call will determine the outcome of the call you make.

A few years ago, I was obsessed with finding answers as to why these patterns take place. Since science did not have answers to it, I thought I would find them myself. So, what I discovered by reading a lot of books on psychology and doing a lot of research in quantum physics. Quantum physics is what gave me the meaning of my thoughts earlier. But then, when I started exploring the quantum world, I realized that everything I was experiencing in my life was defined and explained by quantum physics. According to classical physics, all humans are a separate entity because everybody has their own individual lives.

Classic physics refers to everybody as an object. Then the question arises as to how things are interconnected with each other. As I quoted in an example earlier, your thoughts before making a sales call will determine the outcome of the call. If you end up getting good results, eventually, your clients will also receive good results. When I was going through a tough time, everyone I met was also going through the same phase as me.

This is how the world is interconnected. Therefore, if you think that you are isolated from the rest of the world, it is just a classic physics view of the world.

Quantum physics on the other hand is how everything works: the best description we have of the nature of the particles that make up matter and the forces with which they interact.

Quantum physics underlies how atoms work, and so why chemistry and biology work as they do. You, me and the gatepost – at some level at least, we're all dancing to the quantum tune. If you want to explain how electrons move through a computer chip, how photons of light get turned to electrical current in a solar panel or amplify themselves in a laser, or even just how the sun keeps burning, you'll need to use quantum physics.

The difficulty and, for physicists, the fun, starts here. To begin with, there's no single quantum theory. There's quantum mechanics, the basic mathematical framework that underpins it all, which was first developed in the 1920s by Niels Bohr, Werner Heisenberg, Erwin Schrödinger and others. It characterizes simple things such as how the position or momentum of a single particle or group of few particles changes over time.

According to classical physics, matter is solid, whereas according to quantum physics, it could be wave or particle based on observation. The double-slit experiment states that when you observe the particles, they do exactly what they are supposed to do based on observer's view of the world. However, when you stop observing them, the particles stop behaving the way we think they are going to behave. The particles seem to be fixed when you observe them, and when you stop, they do whatever they want to do. You will discover more on this topic in chapter 20. I truly believe that everything is interconnected, just like all the particles are interconnected with each other, and the feedback loop is always at work. It depends on you if it is positive or negative.

Chapter 5
Alchemy of Success

"Life is full of mysteries but your identity should not be one of them."

— *Awolumate Samuel*

This chapter is especially for all of you who have been on the journey of personal development, have read a lot of books, and have attended a lot of events. However, you might still be wondering why you have not reached the next level. Why things are not working the way you expect them to?

In this chapter, I will be sharing my experiences in the same field and what I discovered to reach the next level. This is what I like to call Alchemy of Success. Alchemy refers to the process where lead turns into gold. Where things actually happen!

In the previous chapters, we have discussed mindsets and why people are not able to move forward in life because they carry so much baggage. People carry a lot of past events with them in their present life. They tend to think that it has been handled; however, believe it or not, it still lingers around. **The past is always there**

unless you actually deal with it and let go!

Like I've said earlier, we are all living under someone else's story. Maybe someone else must have told them, or maybe they must have talked about it. However, the best thing one can do is to create your own story. We are all aware of the fact that in order to move forward and get to the next level in life, we all need to create our own story. In this chapter, we are going to take action. Let's take a quick look at a scenario here. If you look at the world, people are continuously struggling. And why is that? That is because we have been taught the same thing over and over again. In schools, in colleges, and in universities, students are being taught the same thing. Therefore, the rich people are getting even richer. It doesn't matter how long you have been studying at a university or how hard you are working, the struggle still remains.

Identity Crisis

The reason why people are unable to succeed in life despite their hard work and study is because of *Identity*. This is what creates a hurdle for people to take their lives to another level. And this is where the problem arises. There are people who know what they are supposed to do, yet they do not take any action. This is also one reason why people are not succeeding in life. Identity crisis occurs when you have to completely change yourself in order to achieve your goals and dreams in life.

The transformation you bring to achieve those goals and dreams is not actually you. This new person or new identity is to blame for achieving your goals and dreams. I was a person who studied and worked in technology all my life. Ten years ago, I was a person who was working for all the big corporates. As part of my journey, I worked to understand how human psychology worked. Ten years later, I became the person who ran different businesses, who lead team members as a leader and brought companies to a point where they earned millions. It took me a lot of failures to reach where I am today, and the reason for those failures is an identity crisis. I never had the courage to stand up and speak in front of a crowd, let alone explain my theories to them.

The problem with most people is that they are not willing to let go of their existing identity. If you want to move forward and get to someplace, you must move on from who you are today and evolve into somebody you want to be.

Observer Theory

In reference to the double-slit experiment mentioned in the previous chapter, there is something known as the observer theory. The observer theory is simply where a person is observing a situation or a phenomenon changes the phenomenon. Simply put, the particles work exactly the way that the observer wants them to work.

We are aware that observer theory works in the quantum world, and we know that everything is a particle that is interconnected with each other. Therefore, you can transcend yourself as a new character in your story. So this means that you can create your future based on what you are going through right now. What does all that actually mean? Well, thoughts transcend into a new you.

Tony Robbins always said, *"I created this motherfucker Tony Robbins!"*

There are many other examples in the world today:

J.K Rowling – Before she earned millions, she had to face a failed marriage, being almost entirely broke while raising a child on her own and going to school.

Winston Churchill – He failed his sixth grade because he struggled in school. He failed in politics for many years every time he ran for the public office. At 62, he became the prime minister of UK. He was twice elected as such and was also awarded a Nobel Prize in Literature in the year 1953

Ludwig Van Beethoven – He was very awkward on the violin. His teachers thought he was not brilliant enough but it didn't stop him there. He composed five of best loved symphonies of all time even when he was going deaf

THE FAST GROWTH METHOD

Dr. Seuss – Publishers think his books are not sellable so they rejected him. In fact, 27 of them did. Now, his books are read by Children all over the world.

Michael Jordan – He was kicked out of his high school basketball team. He missed more than 9,000 shots and lost 300 games.

Henry Ford – He was broke five times and his early businesses failed.

Thomas Edison – His teachers said he was "too stupid to learn anything". He got fired from two of his jobs because he was unproductive. His failed 1,000 times with his invention. Now we are using his idea to light our homes.

Only few people transcend themselves in a future state where they picture themselves in the future. These people are the ones who create their own stories. Things might not be working in their life today but the only thing they know and remember is their future self.

So how do you do that? Let's answer a few questions.

- Who are you right now?
- How would you describe yourself?
- How much money do you currently make?
- How do you present yourself?
- What are your bad and good habits?
- What are you good at?

- What are you NOT good at?

What is the purpose of all this? Through this exercise, you are trying to create a new version of yourself. You will understand what elements you need to create a new you. Most people do not understand the importance of doing so. A lot of people make the mistake of trying to achieve their dreams without bringing the necessary changes to their character. These people believe that they can achieve their goals by just working hard. These people get up each morning and work to reach their goals; however, their existing character does not allow them to. The reason is, their existing character does not align with their future character. If you only try to change the behaviour without changing the character, the behaviour won't last after few days. To change the behaviour, you must first change the character.

Now let me ask you this question, what do you really want?

How to Create a Life of Your Dreams?

In order to create a life of your dreams, you need to go through the following steps.

- **Dream:** You need to have a dream.
- **Define your Dream:** Once you have your dream, you will need to define it. For example, you are planning to buy a

house. So you need to define the amount and look for places where you think you will be able to find your dream house in that amount.

- **Do You Really Want To Do It?** This is a question that really gives you an answer to whether or not you really want to achieve that dream of yours. This is the point where you actually make a firm decision.
- **Share It:** The moment you start sharing your dream, you are giving it more energy. You are more enthusiastic about accomplishing it. You are looking for people who understand your dream. Their positive energy can feed that dream and push you to achieve it and take it to the next level.
- **Path:** Once you have the motivation to move forward with your dream, you will have to create a path as to what you need to do to achieve it. i.e. business etc.
- **What is Required?** This is the step where you have to create a game plan and think of the necessities required to achieve your dream. You need to think of the steps you need to take in order to reach your dream.
- **Daily Action:** Of course, you cannot just create a game plan and expect it to work out on its own. You will need to take daily action in order to reach your goals according to the steps that you have created.

- **Quantum Mind Meditation:** Daily practice of Quantum Mind Meditation to transcend you into the new character. (more on this in chapter 20)

As part of the above exercise, I would recommend that you write down what you feel your future character will be like. Think of the person who will work to achieve that goal. It's obvious that it is not the person that you are today. Because if you were that person, you would have achieved your goal a long time ago. For example, today, if you are somebody who is not comfortable speaking in public, your future, you will be completely comfortable in doing so.

In order for you to become the person that you dream of being, you need to identify the differences between the two personalities. You need to understand the reason for the gap in between them and identify the character changes you need to make in order to become the future you that you want to be. Determine the skill sets that you do not have today and work on acquiring them with time.

I'll give you my example. I was an IT guy, and deciding to become a business coach and teach about business. I went through the biggest identity crisis. My biggest identity was that I was never the person who could speak in public. But then, I took the decision to become this future me, and that is when I got the ability to speak, to teach, to talk, make videos, etc. Therefore, I turned to Quantum mind meditation and any meditation that I did, I transcended myself from the previous person to the person I have become today (more on this in chapter 20). Technically, I created all those particles in my brain, which are aligned with my future self. I had to overcome my fears, learn some skills, and then reach to the place where I am today.

One piece of advice that I want to give is to consciously create your character. I consciously created my character, and I wanted to be the person that I am today. You need to consciously create your own story because people mostly believe that they are characters in other people's stories. They believe that somebody else is writing their story, and they are just playing their roles in it. I personally think that the actual fun starts when you take a pen and write your own story where you play the main character.

Yes, become your own superhero!

Creating Your Own Story

If you are someone who is looking to write your own story, I would personally recommend that you start putting in the effort to do so. You can begin by taking photographs today. You do not have to show them to people. You can simply take them for yourself. When you start walking towards your dream, take photos to record your journey. Also, observe those photos and try to pinpoint what you are doing right or wrong. That way, you can learn from your mistakes and correct them yourselves. After some time, when you reach your goal, these photos would become interesting to share with others as they carry an entire story with them. To summarize the chapter, remember that staying in the same character and working to achieve goals is a mistake that people make all the time.

Successful people define their new character and build themselves into the new character in order to achieve their goals and dreams. Lastly, I will leave you with an exercise to picture what your future character will look like. Think of it and create it consciously.

(I run an event called Quantum Mind Experience in Australia, which is exactly what we talked about in this chapter. Helping people create their future identity particle by particle using Quantum Mind meditation practices)

Chapter 6
Momento Homo

"The greatest legacy one can pass on to one's children and grandchildren is not money or other material things accumulated in one's life, but rather a legacy of character and faith"

- Billy Graham

In this chapter, I would like to discuss a concept known as *"Memento Homo."* The concept arose from a story in Roman history. There was once a Roman man, or you can say, slave, who was specifically hired to do only one job. This man's name was Auriga. He was hired by the Kings of that time. He would repeat one word to all the Kings of that time. That word was *"Memento Homo."*

These words translated to *"Remember you are only human!"* The reason I am sharing this story with you is to advise you that no matter how successful you may be or how rich you become, you need to keep in mind that you are only human. We are all just humans. So, you need to apply these ethics in the right way to build something consistent and ethical. Most importantly, do not let that egoistic mind come in the middle of your success.

Moreover, in this chapter, I would also like to talk about the probability theory and stats. What is the probability theory? It basically means the chances are 50-50. Anything you do, the outcomes are 50-50. For example, if you flip a coin, the chances are 50-50 that it might either be heads or tails. This is the way the probability theory works. If you take a look at today's world, society is based on statistics. For example, 90% of small businesses tend to fail in the first 12 months. 60% of marriages fail in the first 2 years, and 40% of kids raised by single parents end up going to jail, etc. In today's world, people have started believing in statistics and probability theory. And that is where the problem starts. Now let's take the example of playing cards. When you are playing cards, cards have no knowledge or any skill set on their own. They are simply papers that are used to play. These cards have no capacity to make a decision on how they are going to affect the game. In the same way, most people run their lives based on stats. People imagine themselves as cards, thinking that they do not have the capacity to cause an impact.

People tend to forget that they have the ability to change and to bring a change. They forget that they have the ability to change an outcome. However, people think that they are simply the person who is doing what they have to because they do not have any other choice. And sometimes, the belief of such people is so true. This is the biggest weakness in today's world.

THE FAST GROWTH METHOD

This is where I got my biggest breakthrough. No matter what the truth is, it all comes down to **what we believe in**. It all depends on the perception of the people. When you are running a business, people tend to think that whatever they believe in, eventually, everyone else has to believe in the same theory. What people do not understand is that when they work with the belief that is what shapes their reality.

So here is how it goes. If you have a belief, it becomes a reality. That reality then becomes a stronger belief, which turns to a stronger reality. That is where the feedback loop starts and keeps going. Let me quote an example. A good friend of mine was so unfortunate that she always ended up in a relationship where the person would pass away. Her first husband passed away, so did her second. She met a guy after a while, and after being in a relationship with him for six months, she learned that he was diagnosed with cancer.

That person eventually passed away too. She got into another relationship after some time, and the same thing happened to that guy. Most people would think that the girl has some evil spirit or something. However, what I think is that because of her belief, she ended up meeting people who had a high probability of dying early. People would not get sick after meeting her, and they might have been sick before meeting her. But her beliefs made her attract people who are sick.

This is what most people think that their surroundings have an impact on their lives. However, it is the beliefs that end up causing an impact on their lives. People make the mistake of changing their reality without having to change their beliefs. When we change our beliefs, we begin changing our reality. The moment that you think you need to change your beliefs, then that is when your reality changes because without that, your reality will never change.

Life is not like playing cards where you play a good game when you have good cards in your hand. In life, you have control. I would like to share my story of when I first started in the business.

When I started my business, a lot of people had a lot to say. Such as:

- You can't spend that much amount of money on Facebook ads
- Facebook ads do not work
- People do not attend workshops anymore
- You've tried it so many times; it doesn't work
- Your business relies on people too much
- You could have done anything, why this?
- People are racists; they won't come to your workshops
- People never make money in the education world

This is what people do. They give you their world view and their experiences. As a result, people take those world views and make them their reality. I am not saying that you don't listen to people, what I am saying is that don't leave your path and your dreams as well as your goals because of someone's view of the world. For example, someone tells you that Facebook ads don't work. You may give a try, but the minute it doesn't work, you would be ready to give up. That is how the feedback loop starts. Therefore, since you don't believe in Facebook ads, the next time you try again, it just won't give enough outcome. All because of your belief. Facebook ad is just an example. Let look at any food. If you believe that eating fish would give you freckles. Trust me, after a month or two of eating fish couple of times a week you will start to see freckles on your face.

For most people, the feedback loop works in a negative way. Whereas for some people, it works in a positive way. These are the people who understand the feedback loop. They are aware that the moment they change the feedback, their loop will be in a positive way. They also work to ensure that their loop doesn't end up in a negative way.

Creating a Separate Character

Most people think that their character is controlled by someone else or by some other circumstances. They are controlled by somebody else. Some may even believe that God is doing everything for them or to them, and they blame God for things that are not working out. Some may even blame outsiders or random people for their situation. But what they forget is that the only person to blame is themselves. They are the character. When you observe your life as a third person or as an outsider, you are observing everything. You observe yourself as a separate character.

You are not the person who is taking action. Instead, you are just part of the character. This character today is based on the theories and thoughts that you have been fed throughout your life. Some of the things that you did or you are doing have been taken from other people. Now what you have to do is to build this character based on your new beliefs. This concept is known as Observer Theory. I want you to start observing your life. Think of it like you are playing a video game and that video game is your life. Buddha introduced this concept around 2500 years ago, where he instructed us to observe breathing, and the other thing was to observe the mind. What Buddha meant was that the mind is the character of your movie. So if you are annoyed, observe yourself being annoyed. You do not have to associate everything with yourself. Buddha's theory suggested that you need to get out of this space and observe everything as an outsider. Therefore, you are not experiencing anything; rather, you are just observing it. Lao Tzu came with a similar concept at the same time that Buddha did.

Although these are two very different entities, yet they emerged with the same concept. Lao Tzu introduced Taoism with certain rules. One of the rules is to observe nature and observe the mind. Look at things as an external character, and don't become a part of it. When you are living within your character, you end up with fear and anxiety. Therefore, when you meet people who are enlightened and happy and motivated, they do not have any fear nor anxiety, nor worries.

Why? Because they do not live in character, they observe it and bring the necessary changes. If the character does not have certain skills, they do things to make the character develop those certain skills. Everything can be learned, and you can always add new skills to your character whenever needed. When building your own character, your emotions may take over you. For example, whenever I wanted to start something different, my emotions would take over me. So, you may be wondering how to control those feelings or emotions?

You might have realized that kids are pretty persuasive when they do not want to do anything. For example, if they don't want to go to school, they are going to cry and scream that they do not want to go to school. What do you do? Most parents end up saying, *"Just do it," "we have to do it," "you don't have a choice."* Some parents may even bribe their kids to go to school. You know how to deal with it. Why? Because you are observing it, and not participating in it.

In the last 4 years of my life, I myself have gone through a lot as a person to change my character. I had to take the step and develop this new character. Before I started doing what I do today, I was a pretty shy guy who had zero public speaking skills. My previous character controlled, pretty much, everything. What I had to do was fight back to create a new character if I had to become the person I am today.

If we look at the software versions, every year they come up with a newer and advanced version as compared to the previous one. The newer version has new features and a new way of doing things and solving our problems. This means evolving into a new character. Whenever I started my business, I would look at different competitions and would end up being sick. I got scared, and I was not able to focus and succeed. I would compare my level with others and would just fall sick and lose all hope. I created a new pattern of starting my business. I started with simple market research, after which I developed my business model. After I built my business model, I moved forward to discussing sales and then revenue. This new pattern allowed me to make the changes I needed in order to survive in the business market.

Who is the Boss?

I would like to share my example of when I got my first dog. I took him to puppy classes when he was 18-weeks-old. I remember whenever I would give him something and try to take it back, he would growl at me. That growling scared me and got me worried that if he would do the same when he would grow up. That is when the instructor came to me and told me that I had to show him WHO IS THE BOSS. She said, *"If you are scared now, the dog will make sure that you stay scared of him all your life. You need to be firm and show him who the boss is"*.

After that, I worked on taking over and being the owner of my dog. Your mind is exactly like that. You need to show your mind who's boss. You cannot let your mind take over you. You need to be able to tell your character to perform and play its part. You want to be the character that is evolving with time. For example, today, wealth is nothing but a standard for me. I've seen people who chase wealth and work really hard for it. Some people even believe that they are entitled for more wealth, which is why they don't have it. For my current character, it is just a standard.

Therefore, you need to decide what your character needs to have. You are the one writing the story. The bottom line is, the person you are today cannot achieve your goals. So you need to become somebody else. You are not the same person you were 5 years ago; in fact, you are a better version of yourself. In IT, to get the next software version, new programming is required. Without new programming, new software cannot be obtained.

In the same way, people need to be newly programmed in order to get the new version of themselves. Self is nothing but a character that is moving towards its next version. Everyone is working towards improving themselves. They are working on improving the existing software but not thinking of reprogramming it. This is the biggest flaw in Western education.

In the end, you are becoming something. However, the question is, what are you becoming?

Chapter 7
What are you becoming?

"For me, becoming isn't about arriving somewhere or achieving a certain aim. I see it instead as forward motion, a means of evolving, a way to reach continuously toward a better self. The journey doesn't end."

— ***Michelle Obama***

To continue on the topic that was previously discussed, I ask you again, ***what are you becoming?*** Your answer needs to be simple and a one-liner. It should define what you want to be known for. When people hear your name, what do you want to be known for in their perception?

A lot of people have shared their concerns with me regarding what if they plan on changing who they want to be in the next few years. And I agree with that. If one achieves his/her goals and succeeds, it does not mean that he/she stops there. In fact, you should move on to achieve the next goal. Life is an evolution, and we will always work to reach the next level.

I'm not here to design your life for the next fifty years. I am only designing your character for the next few years. When creating a character for yourself, do not focus on the features first (yet). Take things step-by-step. The first step you take should be what you want to do.

Let me give an example of Superman. What is he designed to do? He is known to fight crime. Similarly, Spiderman is also known to fight crime as well. Why do we have cars? The only reason cars are designed is to take you from point A to point B. There may be a lot of features that are really good in a car, such as its comfy seats, smooth drive, etc., but if the car is not able to do what it is designed to do, the car is useless. What about a refrigerator? What is it used for? Its basic purpose is to keep things cool. A fridge may have a lot of features worth mentioning, but if it does not keep things cool, then what use is it of?

So Jag? What are you becoming? I'm becoming a *Fast Growth Authority*. I am becoming that person who helps people to take their life and business to the next level *FAST!*

Next, I want you to start thinking about your superpower. What is your superpower? Take the above examples, Superman, Spiderman, cars, fridge; each one has a unique superpower. For example, Rolls Royce and Ford have their own set of superpowers. These superpowers are what differentiate them from the rest. Spiderman and Superman, both fight crime. However, they both have very different superpowers.

Superman has the powers of flight, superhuman strength, x-ray vision, heat vision, cold breath, super-speed, and enhanced hearing, whereas Spiderman has precognitive spider-sense ability. A fridge's superpower is its compressor. If it does not have a compressor, it won't work. When we are talking about cars, their features can be many things. It can be the engine power, the brand, the performance, anything.

My Superpower

So many of you know me as the Fast Growth Authority. If you want to scale your business or life *FAST*, you look for Jag. However, what I haven't talked about is my superpower. My superpower is I help transform Monkey Mind into Quantum Mind. This is my superpower, but I know no one will care about the superpower as long as I can help them achieve their goals and dreams. I have learned that nobody has a business problem; instead, everybody has people problems. These problems get reflected in their business.

I understand personal problems. So, if I take people to the next level by helping them transform their Monkey Mind to Quantum Mind, the business itself will grow. This is because I work to grow the business owner and not the business. Frankly speaking, if the strategy was the only thing lacking, then a lot of people would be billionaires today. Sadly, that is not the case.

How to Program?

In the previous chapter, I have mentioned reprogramming yourself into a new character who can achieve your goals and dreams. Most people make the mistake of trying to get everything where they are today. However, they are unaware that the character that they are today will not help them in getting what they are aiming for. So, if you develop that character, everything else will fall into place automatically.

Synchronicity

What is synchronicity? Synchronicity is when certain things happen because you align your mind in a certain way. If you believe that certain things can happen, things are going to align their way according to your thought.

Classic physics says that there is a physical chair. However, how can you confirm that without observing it? If I leave the room and the chair is still present in the room, then how can I confirm that the chair still exists even when I'm not in the room? This is what classic physics implies. However, the quantum world speaks about it differently. It claims that if you do not observe it, you can't confirm if the object actually exists. (Schrödinger's Cat experiment)

Confirmation Bias

It says that one sees things to support existing beliefs. We all do that. We believe in something and see things in a way that things automatically align with what we believe in. For example, if you do not believe that your story is good, you will align yourself with 10 other people who will give you confirmation that your story is not up to the mark.

Confirmation bias states that whatever is internal is what is depicted externally. The way you believe about something, you will ultimately see it happening externally as well. If you believe that you will not succeed in your business, you will definitely see the confirmation bias externally.

All my life, I believed that I would never be good at speaking the English language and I kept receiving the confirmation bias all the time from people associated with me. Let's look at the example of September 11 attack on the twin tower. If you believe that the government was somehow involved in the attack. All external situations will give you confirmation about your belief.

Let's do an experiment. If you believe in something, try unbelieving it for a month. For example, the moon landing. If you are one who believed in it, start unbelieving it. If you think that the moon landing took place, then start thinking that it did not take place. Once you start unbelieving it, observe your environment.

You will notice that your surroundings are giving the confirmation bias of your thought. In the same way, if you are a Trump supporter, you will view his policies to be positive. On the other hand, if you are not his supporter, his policies will always be negative for you, even if they are helpful. The only negative part about confirmation bias is that people who believe in something are not open to hearing the negative aspect of it. They are determined to make their beliefs true.

This is a mistake that we all do. We stay in that belief for such a long time and so strongly that we start to see things that prove those beliefs to be true. That is when the feedback loop starts. Once the feedback loop starts, it becomes hard to get out of it.

Create a Hypothesis

When you understand the quantum mind and enter the meditating world, you start to create a hypothesis for yourself. The next step is that your synchronicity and confirmation biasedness will kick in. Let's do an exercise together. For the next 21 days, repeat the following sentences for yourself and believe in them:

THE FAST GROWTH METHOD

- The Fast Growth Method is helping me grow my business *Fast*
- I am becoming _____
- I am unstoppable
- I am great at selling
- I am going to be amazing at _____

As you start to believe in these statements, you will notice that your synchronicity and confirmation bias will start to kick in and support your beliefs.

How to Program the Mind?

The mind goes through a process to change a belief into action.

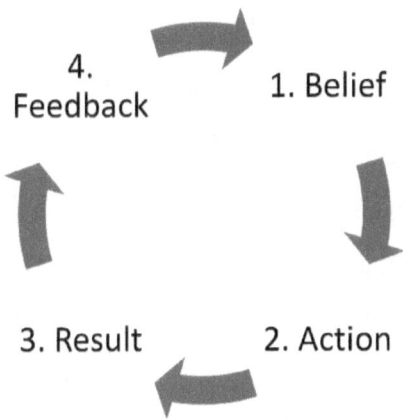

You start with a belief. You believe in something which eventually becomes your action. As you carry out the action, you start getting the results. These results bring in feedback, which then becomes a confirmation of your belief, and the loop goes on.

After you have created a belief and conducted an action and have gotten the result, if there is a delay in the feedback, the loop becomes negative. People make the mistake of believing that when they become someone, then they start taking action. However, the right thing is that you need to start taking action in order to become someone. To become a character, you need to start working for it. When one changes his wants to standards, then that is when the new character is created.

It is a habit of people to start something and eventually stop doing it. This is what brings a halt to achieving dreams and goals. One needs to create a personality or a character so he can start working on it instead of abruptly stopping it in the middle.

I would suggest changing at least one thing in yourself in order to create a new character. You need to discover that one thing which will have an impact on your other personality traits and will help you in creating a new character. Lastly and more importantly, this one thing will help you in achieving your dreams and goals for the long-term.

Chapter 8
How To Achieve Your New Character!

"The important thing is this: to be able at any moment to sacrifice what we are for what we could become."

— *Charles Du Bos*

When you started reading this book, you had a view of the world. What I have been aiming for, is to change that view of the world and give you a paradigm shift. Like I have mentioned many times earlier in the book that we are all living with a view of the world that has been passed on to us by family, friends, and our peers. I am working toward you creating your own view and seeing the world from your new perspective instead of someone else's.

Now that you are moving towards a new character and a new person, there may be a lot of concerns and questions in your head. During this process, if you are confused and unsure of what to do next, you are not alone. You are unsure of which path to walk in and what goal to achieve. This is what I have seen when you get a new view of the world, you begin to see a lot of options and opportunities.

You get confused about which option to pick. The answer to that is very simple, pick the character and it will pick the option.

During my live sessions, a lot of people come up with questions asking if I am referring to building a personal brand. No. I am not referring to building your own brand. I am referring to understanding your own character and what you really want to become.

Present state   Future state

If you look at the above image. As a rule of thumb, the person who help their clients fill the above gap quicker & faster makes most of the money in the marketplace. For example, a person decides that he wants to lose weight. So present state would be 120kg, and future state 80kg and the gap is -40kg. Now there are many ways to go about this. This person can buy a gym membership for $500/annum and lose weight in 12 months.

But what if this person wants to lose weight faster? He can hire a personal trainer for $2,000 and lose weight in 6 months. What if he wants to lose weight in 3 months? He can also hire a nutritionist for another $2,000 and lose weight in 3 months. Similarly, if he wants to lose weight even faster, he can always go to the plastic surgeon and pay $10,000 and get slim in 7 days. Therefore, the person who is able to fill the gap quicker & faster makes most of the money. In this case, the plastic surgeon is able to fill the gap faster and therefore he earns a lot.

Why People Buy?

Whether it is you or your clients, we all wake up in the morning to walk towards our desired future. Each person has certain wants that they want to achieve or certain pain that they want to get away from.

As a business owner, you need to identify that gap in your clientele. What does your client want? Or what are they trying to get away from? And how are you going to fill that gap? Every business present in the market is working to fill a gap.

Once you have successfully identified the gap, you can then help your client in getting to their destination quicker and faster than others while charging more money for it. If you run a consultancy firm, clients come to you with their problems. They tend to have a situation where they are facing a problem while having the urge to fulfill their desired goal(s). If you help them in reaching their desired goal(s) quicker and faster, you will see a massive shift in your business.

Needs vs. Wants

This is a concept that you must understand really well. The first point to understand is that you do not make much money if you are selling those goods which are classified as *needs*. Most people believe that they need to be in the 'needs' category to make money. For example, bread and butter are in the needs category, and the prices of such commodities are still almost the same as 10 years ago. Therefore, it is important to understand whether you are selling needs or wants.

Secondly, one must learn to move the product from needs to wants because most of the people spend their time talking about their wants. If you are fixing a pain, you are in the need industry because people need you at that time. If I've broken my back, I need to fix it. That is not a want; it is a need. For example, people would pay $40 for a pain relief massage because they need it in time of pain. However, if people will opt for a wellness massage, they will have to pay $250. Wellness massage is a want and not a need. It is a luxury service that is required but not necessarily needed. When you visit a high-end hotel, they will treat you with a wellness massage in order to earn more money. Why? The answer is because people pay more for wants. They do not pay more for needs. In your clients view of the world, they must see your products or services as 'needs'. For example: I *need* access to Jag's 'Champions Club Program' to reach 50K a month revenue.

If you have a business, it is now the best time to go back and think which is the biggest gap that you have filled? If you are running a cleaning service business, people come to you to get their house/car cleaned. In that case, what kind of gap are you filling? You are helping people in filling the gap cleaning their houses. Since you are filling the gap, it means that you are taking away the pain from them. That is what you are doing as a business.

Now I'm going to move towards something that is totally different. This is about a concept that I learned a few years ago when things were not working out in my life. Since day one, I have been made to be an employee. Everyone that I have ever been associated with, i.e. my uncles, aunts, relatives, and teachers were all employees. I have completed my Postgraduate in Management, done my Masters in IT and have also completed a number of different courses. All these courses and programs have been taught by different employees. Therefore, there weren't any business people who would teach me things under the context of business.

Later on in life, I started hanging out with business owners. That is when I started understanding the different principles of business and its terminologies. The biggest influence on my life has always been Ray Dalio (principles.com). Some of the teachings he taught completely changed my view of the world. According to Ray, there are three fundamentals in the marketplace; skillset, market, and product/service.

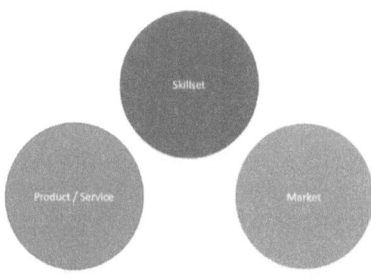

There are two stages of the employee mindset. *Stage 1* is the system that teaches the student or employee that he needs to work on a skillset. Most people start at this level. I started with gaining my bachelor's degree, then my postgrad, then masters, and then different certification programs. I worked on improving my skillset. Once the student gains his skillset and takes those skills to the market, he feels that he is entitled to get a job because he has more skills than the rest. However, the market refuses to give him a job because there are no jobs. This makes him furious and angry. Then there is *Stage 2*. Stage 2 is basically where you are better at something, and with the help of that skill, you open up your own business. The employee starts the same way by gaining all the education and the skill-set needed. Then he opens up his own business and enters the market. As a result, the market responds by saying they do not need such a service. Then again, you become infuriated and mad. The last one is entrepreneurial mindset

This mindset asks three questions. The first question, *"What does the market want?"* It is about studying the market and understanding what is it in need of. Once you understand the market needs, you then need to look for a product or service to fulfill the demand or fill the gap. The second question, *"What product/service do I need to fill that gap?"* To produce this product, the entrepreneur needs to decide whether he/she possesses the required skillset or if he/she has to hire someone else to do it. The third question, *"Do I have this skillset, or can I hire someone else?"*

This is very important concept so I want to make sure you understand this really well. Don't make the mistake which most people make. Spend time on doing research in the market to understand *what does my market want? What product / service do I need to fill that gap?* And the last one *"do I have the skillset or do I need to hire someone"*. This is very different from, *I have done accounting degree and now I will start an accounting business.*

Jim Rohn quoted, *"We get paid for bringing value to the marketplace."* I never understood what *"value"* is and how I would define *"value."* I understood that I needed to work harder and give more or similar to what I was already giving. However, as I delivered more and more, I realized that I was not being paid or rewarded according to the amount of work that I was giving. The reason for this was that nobody taught me the *"Value Ladder."*

Value Ladder

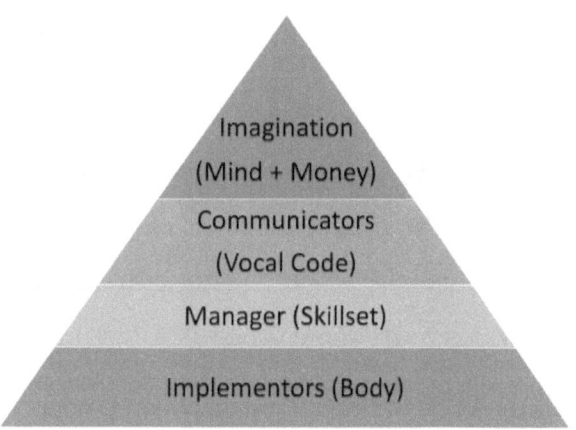

This could be the most important thing you will learn in this book. The bottom-most level is where the implementers are. These people are those who do things for you. These people include waiters, road makers, and labors. They use their *bodies* as a tool for work. For people at this level, their wage does not increase dramatically no matter the amount of work they do. They might just get $1,000 - $5,000 increase per annum.

THE FAST GROWTH METHOD

The second step on the ladder is where the managers are. This level includes the people who make money with the help of their *skillset*. They use their skillset as a tool. For example, I worked as a tech expert during my early days and used my skillset to earn money. I stayed at this level for the longest period of time. I worked really hard, yet I only got a $5,000 - $10,000 increase per annum. I never understand this earlier that why I wasn't making more money, even though I am working really hard and providing more value to my clients. People think that they can add more value and make more money by staying at the same level on the ladder. However, this thought is rather incorrect. The best way to add value and make more money is by jumping to the next step of the ladder.

On the third step of the value-ladder are the communicators. These people add value and earn money with the help of their *vocal code*. The increase in demand for people at this level is really high as compared to the previous two levels. These people include movie stars, singers, public speakers, etc. The best you can do in your industry is to become a communicator. The people who stand up and speak makes way more money than those who sit and listen.

The topmost level on the value ladder is imagination. This includes the people who use their imagination to make money. These people have two tools to earn money. One is they have the mind to earn money, and second is they have the money to make more money. These are those people who created things that are based on their imagination. Steve Jobs and Bill Gates are the biggest examples of imaginations.

Most people do not make more money in life because they are on the wrong spot on the value ladder. Why? The answer is because they believe that they are going to work hard while staying on the same spot and make money. As mentioned earlier, this is not how it works. You need to jump to different spots on the ladder in order to make more money.

One major reason why people fail is that they replay their stories in their heads and they get into the feedback loop. While they are replaying the stories, they overthink, and therefore, they lose motivation to do things better. To get out of this feedback loop, one has to understand that he has control over it. In order to become successful, you need to change into the person who deserves that success. If you do not do that, you are just standing in the same place, striving for something that will not be achieved. They try to achieve things while maintaining the same character. After some time, that character takes over the person and life runs on autopilot. Who knows someone like this?

How do you achieve your new character? You can start by taking note of your daily rituals. Once you have done that, imagine the daily rituals of your new character. Here's the 'aha' moment, start working on daily rituals of your new character. If you want to be the best public speaker, what does the best public speaker do every day? The best way to find out is to ask someone who you believe is where you want to be so you can model their daily rituals.

Someone asked Dan Brown (the famous author) how much does he write every day? He responded, 4-6 hrs. every day. So now the question is - he is Dan Brown that's why he writes 4-6 hrs. every day or he has been writing 4-6 hrs. every day that's why he is Dan Brown?

Chapter 9
Wealth Opportunities

"Wealth is the ability to fully experience life."

- **Henry David Thoreau**

In this chapter, we will be discussing wealth. As we live in a society, we all need to start thinking and talking about money. Therefore, this chapter will be all about wealth opportunities, how to look for them, why people are unable to see them, and how are we going to create wealth.

I started from the very beginning. I was not the person who inherited money from my parents. No. My mother didn't pay for my university fee or my food or living expenses. I was working part time when I was studying at the university. Slowly and gradually, here I am now doing what I do.

I truly believe that if these teachings are not passed on to the generation, this practice will not be done by the upcoming youth. Even they will have to start from the beginning. All I'm saying is that not everyone has to go through the troubles we have and start from zero. We can all help others and teach them the skills, so they do not have to think about money the way we once thought of it.

There are two ways of how people see the world. One is the wealth mindset, where they see wealth and opportunities everywhere. Whatever they look at, they find things in abundance. The other way is the lack mindset where they face a lack of time, lack of money, and lack of opportunities everywhere they go. A few chapters back, I mentioned getting yourself in patterns, and I asked you to ponder over the patterns that you have been running in your life. Now I need you to focus on what sort of money pattern have you been running. Have you been running a pattern where you have trained your mind to believe that there is a lack in the world? money is the root of all evil? Or you are not skilled enough to make more money?

It is so weird that there is so much money sitting in the banks, and they are so alike. There is no difference between a 100 dollar bill in a bank in Brisbane and another 100 dollar bill in a bank in Sydney. As per the marketing rule, whatever is in abundance in the market, thus the demand decreases. And what we do not have today is people like you and I. There is no other you. When things are not the replica of each other, they are unique, and people pay high prices for these products.

We need to own up to the fact that we are the only people in the world. We, human beings, have all it takes to make money if we really want to. However, what barriers come in between? A small thing called "belief" comes in the middle. It doesn't matter what you teach to others; it is important to believe in it and apply it to yourself. According to my belief, if you do not have enough money today, it is because you do not have a wealthy character.

Going back to the lack mindset, it is where someone says No to every opportunity that comes knocking their door. The way they assess any opportunity is by looking at their existing character. These people have less money in hand and in their bank accounts too. The reason behind this could be that they are making money; however, they are spending too much. If you are one of those who is caught in such a situation, all I want is for you to come out of that loop. Schools, colleges, and universities have given us the mindset that we are all meant to earn fixed incomes and limits i.e. accountants make $120K or IT consultant makes 130K. However, the wealth mindset states that there should not be a limit. All I am saying is that you need to catch yourself if you believe that you have fixed income bracket.

Wealth mindset is where people always say Yes to new opportunities (at least until they've made their first million). They look at everything with abundance, and the most important is that they look at opportunities and know how to assess them. Their mindset and the way they look at the world, they see it with abundance and curiosity.

How to Create Unlimited Opportunities?

I wear glasses, and I see things pretty clearly with my glasses on, but if I take my glasses off and look around, everything is blurry. The same issue is with most people. When they do not have their abundance glasses on, they are not able to see clearly. Therefore, they are not able to see opportunities around them. The question is, how does one see opportunity?

Tap into Your Curiosity

Every human being was born curious. They are curious to know about everything and find out about things. We ask a lot of questions and try to understand what is going around us. One characteristic that I have found in billionaires is that they are always curious. They want to know about things and how it works. The problem is we are always taught in schools, colleges, and universities about the importance of skill sets. And then as time passes by, we end up talking only about those skill sets. The curiosity fades away, and all that is left is skill set. You end up talking and knowing only about your skill sets, and everything else does not matter anymore.

People today are not able to make money because they are emotionally attached to the solution. These people love what they do because they have been doing it for so long. It is not because they really want to do it, but it is because they have done it for so long that they are skilled in that particular profession. Hence, everything revolves around what they do. They don't want to hear anything new.

Curiosity

Do you know how the pizza saver was born?

In 1916, New York, a man hated it when his pizza was ruined when the delivery boy brought it to him. The pizza box would ruin the pizza by the time he received it. That's when he came up with the pizza saver. This tiny little triangle turned into a 10 million empire, and currently it is a 26 million dollar company. Each pizza saver is sold for 10 cents each.

THE FAST GROWTH METHOD

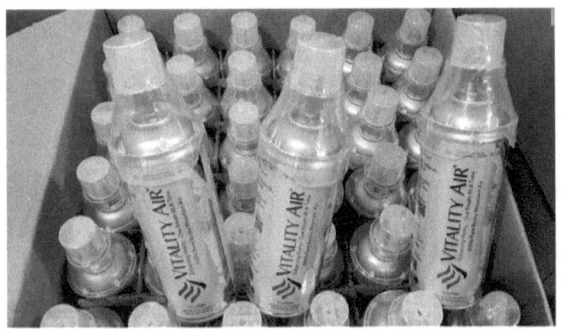

Vitality Air, a Canadian company that sells canned air

Two guys in Canada collected air in a bottle and shipped it to China by the name Vitality Air. They practically sold Canada Air in a can and is now making $230,000 annually. ***Curiosity leads to money***. When you buy a pizza, it costs you $10-$12. On the other hand, if you sell one slice for $5 and each pizza has 8 slices, you sell it for $40 a pizza.

Language of Money

The language of money is math. All you need is to speak that language. By language, I mean *"I can get this for $____ and sell it for $____, then I have an opportunity!"* Sometimes people think of ideas that the market does not need. Billionaires out there have multiple streams of income, which is why they do not have a money problem. This is where you need to think of the number of opportunities that can give you money. Most people are not made to make money due to our system.

The reason is that they think of their skillset and decide what they need to sell. These people get confused when any other opportunity comes because they are not aware of how to evaluate that opportunity and how to do the math to avail that opportunity. So here I ask you one question, *"If you can pick one personality trait to make more money, what would that be?"* Would the answer be something along the lines of honest, hardworking, or learning more about computers? I would recommend *consciousness*. Consciousness is about being aware of what is going on around you. When running a business, you need to wear many hats and have a number of different skill sets. However, one trait that has helped me and many other millionaires around me is consciousness. All the millionaires have a lot of consciousness. They are aware of what is going on around them and in the market.

How to Train Your Consciousness

You must learn to *focus*.

I'd like to make the argument that focus is the most critical component when it comes to developing your consciousness.

When Steve Jobs famously came back to Apple in 1997, was his first mandate to make the iPod or iPhone? No!

How many people know that Jobs spent four years cutting unsuccessful products, reducing costs and improving operations with Tim Cook, Apple's COO (now CEO) — before he ever released the iPod? He got EVERYTHING else out of the way before Apple could start innovating again. He reduced Apple products by 70 percent.

The number one focus killing factor today is smartphone notifications. Make sure to turn them off. When you get a notification for anything, you get a dopamine hit. This dopamine hit creates a neurotransmitter. Humans have receptors in the brain, and these receptors disturb the pattern of the neurotransmitters. When this happens, you become less focused or less conscious.

Success is a Gradual Process, Not Linear

When I was in college, I wanted to make lot of money. Money was my biggest drive for anything. It didn't matter if I wanted to do business or anything, I simply wanted to make a lot of money. My belief was I needed to make a million dollars, and the results came out that I made only $25,000. I tried a few times and kept trying; however, the increase was only $10,000, $15,000, or $20,000. The increase was very minor.

This gave me wrong feedback, which created my belief that I cannot make money. That is when I understood that success is a gradual process. If you work on the character (identity) which makes more money than it become easier and normal to have money. The problem comes when people don't change the character and try very hard to make more money while living in the same identity.

How Businesses are making Money?

If businesses are making money today it is because they are just financially curious. They understand how to make money. So now the question here is, are you financially curious? Are you trying to find new ways to make money in your business, or you just following the same old business model followed by pretty much everyone in your industry? The moment you are curious, you start getting the answers.

Millionaires and billionaires are not superhumans. One trait that made them rich today is their *curiosity*. They try to find out what exactly is going on in the marketplace. These people read financial history books. History may not repeat itself, but one can learn a lot by understanding what happened back then.

In the business, you must be a Scientist and not an Artist. One should become a mad scientist. Find different solutions to problems. If one solution does not work, look for another one. In the same way, if one business idea does not work, move on to another one. Experiment with different things and find out which works the best for you. In marketing we are always split testing. There isn't any time in our business when we are not split testing. We are split testing the ad copies, images, videos, landing pages on continuous

THE FAST GROWTH METHOD

basis.

Let me quote a quick story about a frog and a scorpion. I heard this story a while back, and it seems interesting to share. There's a frog that lives in a pond, and a scorpion comes on the side of the pond and asks the frog, *"I want to cross the pond, can you take me there?"* The frog replies, *"You are a scorpion. If I take you to the other side, you might sting me."* The scorpion then replies, *"I cannot do that because if I'm on your back and I sting you, you will drown and I will die as well."*

So the frog decides to take the scorpion to the other side of the pond. While the scorpion was riding the back of the frog, he stung the frog. Before dying, the frog asked the scorpion why he stung him. The scorpion replies, *"Because I'm a scorpion and that's what I do."* That is the identity of the scorpion.

In the same way, we are always true to our identity. Most people work on changing behavior, but not identity. That's why they go to gym few days a week and then stop going after some time. Let me rephrase this again here, and if you want to make more money, you must become the person who attracts money!

Chapter 10
Your Future Identity

"What you get by achieving your goals is not as important as what you become by achieving your goals."

- Zig Ziglar

In the previous chapters, we talked about your identity and your present reality. As in where do you currently stand? Everybody on this planet has a desired future that they are walking towards. Any action they do, it is taking them a step forward towards their desired future. However, there is a gap between where they are and where they want to be.

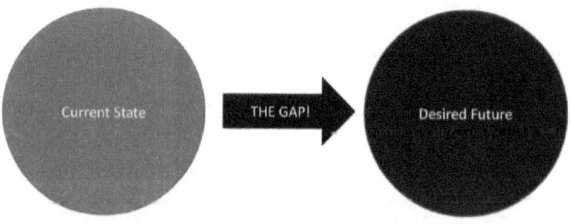

After reading the last few chapters, I'm sure you looked into the mirror to judge where you are and where you are thinking to be in the next few years. You started to see the gap between both these places. Due to that gap, you started feeling little agitated.

Let me tell you this if you are feeling agitated, that means you are in the right place. If you are not feeling agitated, there may be two reasons for it. Either you haven't decided your desired future yet or it means that I haven't done my job properly. However, what I believe is that you haven't decided what you really want. If you haven't decided what you really want, my suggestion would be, put this book down and start thinking. What do you really want? What is your ultimate goal in life?

In this chapter, I will work on developing your future identity. Where you are today and where you want to be. Another thing I want to focus on is the ***Entrepreneur's Trap***. If you are one of those people who are standing here today and working to be someone, you feel a gap. That is when you are caught in the entrepreneur's trap.

This trap has led me to go through many sleepless nights. I have been in that stage where I felt disconnected from the world, from my family, and even disconnected from myself too. I have been under a lot of stress during this trap, and I have experienced feelings like anxiety, anger, and frustration, and many other kinds of negative emotions.

If you are a person who is feeling all these negative emotions, it means you might be part of this trap. I want to make sure that you come out of this trap as quickly as possible. This is a bad trap, especially for the entrepreneurial people. It is also bad for people who are looking to do something to reach some point in life. If a person starts a business and wants to take it somewhere, then this is a big trap for those entrepreneurs. Therefore, I do not want you to be a part of this trap and come out of it ASAP.

I was one of those people and I stayed in that position for a few years. I never realized it, but I was a part of this trap. Therefore, you need to learn to come out of this trap.

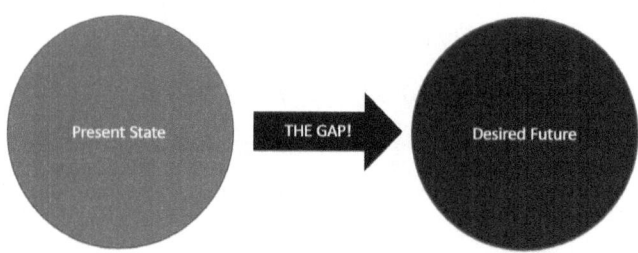

If you haven't realized it by now, there is a gap between where you are today and where you want to be. Some people might have a bigger gap, and some might just have a very tiny gap. Nevertheless, there is a gap. I call this, *"The Gap"* At any point in life, everyone lives in the gap. Even when you are a kid and want to move to the next level, you are in the gap. When you are old, you are looking to move to the next level. It means you are in the gap. Now is the time for an *Aha* moment. ***We are always living in the gap***. And that is where the trap comes in.

At this point, the question to ask you is, are you happy with where you are in life? If your answer is no and you are running away from your present situation, then you will always be running away. That is known as the entrepreneur's trap. Everyone gets caught up in this trap. Why? Because they are not happy with where they are, and they want to run away from it. So how do you know that you are caught in this trap? You start using statements with the If-Then reasoning. So now the question arises, that how many of you want to make more money? How would it feel to be that person? We can all make money and even run businesses if we are that person. For example, you decided that you are going to make $10,000 more than what you are making today. How would that feel?

Look back in the past 10-12 months and try to recall whether you have experienced that feeling. If you haven't felt that feeling in the past 12 months, then you need to ask yourself, *"What is stopping me?"* I have mentioned this earlier as well that the game is an internal game. We want to see things externally first, before feeling them internally. However, this is not how the brain works, and this is definitely not the way the quantum mind works.

A normal human mind only takes information physically from the 5 human senses. We also know that the mind is not able to distinguish between the 5 senses and the imagination. The mind feels exactly the same way, whether you feel it or you imagine it. Therefore, instead of thinking that you are going to feel amazing when you get the money, can you have those feelings right now?

Let's look at now why goal setting doesn't work and what is Modern Goal Setting 2.0

Goal Setting 2.0 - End Goal & Means Goal

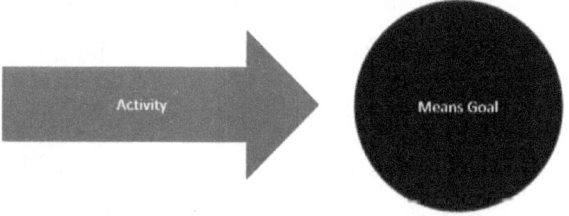

Here's what happens in today's world. We have a goal for something. It may be getting a bachelor's degree, running a certain business, buying a new car, marrying someone, or getting a new job. Everyone has their own 'means goal.' Therefore, they start putting in their efforts and their actions. And when finally, they get to their goal, they start wondering *"Is that all?"* or *"Is that it?"* Look back into your life and think of the time when you wanted something really bad. You worked really hard to achieve that goal, but when you did, there was no special feeling.

You begin thinking *"Is that it?"* So if you have that feeling, then you are a part of this goal setting trap in today's world. Means goal is a goal that define one of many paths to reach your end goals. The end goal is where you want to reach ultimately.

For example, if you complete your bachelor's degree then you will start your master's degree. When you are done with your master's degree, you will work to get a good job. When you have a good job, you will get married. And when you are married, you will be happy. Therefore, being happy is the end goal. What I discovered is that end goal is always some kind of *feeling*.

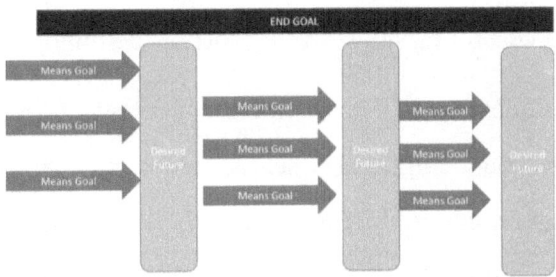

If you go back to the last 12 months of your life, what has been the most important part of your life? For me, learning, growing, success, money, significance, and family were the most important part of my life. I'm sure each one of you has a list of your own. So based on your list, what results have you been able to create out of that? Because you are living that life today which you created 12 months ago, isn't it?

Let me talk about an exercise called the 4F formula;

1. fulfillment,
2. family & friends,
3. finance, and
4. fitness.

I want you to rate the above out of ten by explaining how fulfilled you are in those areas?

With the current identity that you have, what is your big goal today? What does the current person want from life? What feeling does he/she want to feel? Is this person looking to be loved, safe, rich, successful or smart? What sort of feeling does he/she desire?

Next question is, what is the biggest fear of the current identity? Does he fear being broke, scared, not being valued enough or not being loved enough? Another question is, who do I need to be in order to be completely fulfilled with life? Fulfillment is nothing but a feeling. However, what character do you have to be to feel completely fulfilled? What kind of feeling are you looking for?

As homework, I want you to meditate for at least 5 minutes. I need you to close your eyes and imagine the new you. Ask yourself questions such as, who do I need to be in order to feel completely fulfilled? When you are done meditating, ask yourself, what inner conflict do you have about your new identity? Since when you feel completely fulfilled, that's when it is easier to move forward. That fulfillment is what is going to pull you toward your new identity.

You will notice even though you tapped into the new identity only for a few seconds, yet you will feel completely fulfilled. The person who has that feeling and is waking up to that feeling, despite not having the money, the physical material things, but the one big thing that the person is waking up to, is the belief of feeling completely fulfilled.

Can you feel the difference when you step into that new identity? The old me, even though was trying to do everything, was still running away from somewhere. Even though I was making good money, I was still running away from somewhere. The reason is that I wasn't happy in that space, and I didn't feel fulfilled. And I was caught in that entrepreneurial trap that if this happens, then I will be happy. I was living in the If-Then life.

The difference between the old me and the present me is that today I am pretty content, centered, and grounded. I am happy with where I am today. Yes, I have a desired future but I have everything right now as well.

My advice is to *choose* to live with a new identity. Before becoming the new person, you want to bring that person in today's world, step into it, and feel that way too. The point is that we are willing to become a new person by stepping into it and feeling that way. We are working to create your new identity from the place where you are already feeling fulfilled. When you feel fulfilled, you will attract things in the same way.

The most important feeling in life is having an identity who is completely fulfilled where he/she is at…

THE FAST GROWTH METHOD

Path

Chapter 11
The Transition

"Business has only two functions – marketing and innovation."
*– **Peter Drucker***

From this chapter onward, we are going to transition into the business world. I'm going to start with some of the basic fundamentals. I remember my mentor telling me that if I am not able to grow my business and I am stuck in one place, the reason is the foundations are not right. This means that you have not done the work to build the foundation of the business.

You must get the basic fundamentals right. If you are trying to grow a business and you are stuck and don't know how to move forward, it simply means because the basic fundamentals are not clear. In this chapter, I will be talking more about the basic foundations of the business.

One thing I want to be very clear about is that there are no magic pills for the success of the business. You cannot just do one thing and forget the rest. You have to do many things and take many steps for your business to succeed. By now, you must be well-aware that business growth depends on the business owner's growth. Whenever you try to grow, you will always resist it. One thing to understand is that unless there is resistance, growth will not take place. One of my earlier mentors taught me not to run away from resistance. You must embrace resistance in order to grow.

Next, let us quickly discuss what the opposite of the quantum mind is. What is this thing called the monkey mind? You should know that the business will not grow to millions unless you come out of that monkey mind. People who manage to make their businesses successful are out of the monkey mind and are not a part of it. In order to not be a part of it, you need to know the distinctions of this monkey mind.

Here are the top 7 distinctions:

1. I know everything!
2. Social Butterfly - Focused on social interactions instead of results. At every gathering, event, function, thinking this will build their business
3. Try to understand everything intellectually
4. Tell stories (to build the context), instead of asking questions!
5. Blame others (Internet is slow, weather is no good, I am old/young)

6. Not asking for help

7. Shiny object syndrome - Always chasing **shiny objects**

The first distinction of being a monkey mind is claiming that you know everything. If you come to encounter anyone as such, you need to stay away from them because they are going to drag you back into the same space. Some people with a monkey mind are social butterflies, which is why businesses do not seem to flourish as well. These people focus on social interactions rather than results. Most people go out only for the sake of interaction and believing that it will build their business. They are busy giving away their business cards at every event.

They only want to interact with other people so that they can get some business. They do not have results and they do not know how to get their client results. They only like going out and hanging out with other people thinking this will grow their business. They believe that by going out and handing out their business cards can help in building the business. Therefore, they are called social butterfly.

The next one on the list is those people who try to understand everything intellectually. You may remember as we talked about this in earlier chapters. The difference between classic physics and quantum physics. This will certainly not help in growing the business. You must ensure that you are not one of them and you are not trying to do the same. There are times when things will not make sense. You do not have to understand everything. Sometimes, our brain cannot explain things and you have to accept that.

Most people even go out and tell a lot of stories to build the context. For example, you go to a business lunch and ask a question like What do you do? Instead of responding with an answer, people start telling stories. These stories are usually told to try and build the context. People tell a lot of stories as such instead of asking questions. Another trait of people with a monkey mind involves blaming others. They blame the internet for being slow or the weather being not too good, etc. Then there are those who are not used to asking for help. I was one of them, for many years I failed and failed in many businesses but never asked for help. They do things on their own and think they are capable of doing anything and everything.

The last one is people chasing shiny objects every day. If Bitcoin is cool today, they will be talking about Bitcoin. If network marketing is in fashion, they will be bragging about their network marketing business. They have a lot of width experience but no depth in any area.

These are the traits and characteristics of people that have a monkey mind. You need to make sure that you are not part of these people who are doing it. 95% of the people have a habit of doing one or many of these things and being a monkey mind. They do it because they do not understand how the business world works and how the law of nature works.

The monkey mind will be tempted to do everything else except for the thing that is required from them to grow their business. For example, you give people instructions and you tell them what needs to be done before you leave. After you come back, you find out that they ended up cleaning the car, cleaning the house, sending the emails, and everything else, except for what you have instructed them. This is the bad habit of a monkey mind. They know what they need to do, but they find a way to do everything else but not what they were told to.

If you really want to be successful in the business world, you must do what is required. Also, working on your mindset is one thing and doing the work is another thing. What I've noticed through my experiences is that some people just want to do the mindset stuff like meditation and connect with the energy etc. These people are happy doing those things. On the other hand, the other kind of people just look for strategies / steps / processes etc.

You need to be the one to do both because unless you do both, things will not work. You need to have the identity with a quantum mind and not with the monkey mind. The other aspect is that you must have the strategy and you take action. Unless you do the work, the mindset along will not help. And only just doing the work will not help as well. Therefore, you must do both! i.e. Quantum Mind + Action! One thing that has helped me with my success is understanding the principles of the Monkey Mind and the Quantum Mind.

Therefore, start from the quantum mind identity. As mentioned in the previous chapter, you need to create that identity for yourself where the person that you are is completely satisfied with everything that life has to offer. The only way you can lose is *"by giving up"*. One advice that my mentors gave me is to never give up. You need to be willing to do whatever it takes to not give up. Tell yourself that you must take your business to a particular level.

Eventually, you will realize that the only gap you have is the education gap. Everything relies on education. Just because you do not understand how to do it, does not mean that you cannot do it. You can simply get educated about it. People believe that they need a lot of things to make the business successful, however they need only one thing. **Education**. No, I am not saying university degree. I am talking about real life experience. Working with mentors / coaches who have already walked the path you are looking to embark. Remember this, you do not have business problems, you have human problems that get reflected in the business.

I always say that you need to educate the business owner and the business will grow itself.

Always know that things may not work out for the first time. The positive thing you can do is to take it as a feedback and not judge yourself as a failure. Also, you need to understand the difference between strategy and tactics. Strategy is a long-term planning to make things happen, whereas tactics are the steps taken to comply with that strategy. Let me talk about why my businesses failed. You learn from every business. You get feedback from other businesses and therefore, you try to not make the mistakes they did. One of my business failures includes not targeting the right clients. I made the huge mistake of thinking that everyone was my client. I spoke to everybody and tried to understand what they do and market to every other human being. The second mistake I was making was not taking the imperfect action. I kept trying and trying to make things perfect before releasing the products.

Another mistake is taking market feedback personally. I took everything personally. For example, if someone said *"NO"* to me, I would be pissed. Therefore, you need to make sure that you avoid habits as such if you intend to be a successful business owner. Get used to hearing this word "no" because, here's the reality, most people won't buy from you but some will…

Blaming the market instead of learning from the market is

another mistake that I used to do. I used to have this thought that I had so much experience. I worked for big companies and corporations, and I would ask myself why are people not buying from me? When I look back at this habit of mine, I realize how absurd it was to try to sell something, get annoyed as to why it is not being sold, and then blame the market for it.

So, today if you are not growing at the rate that you want to, it means you are not making enough *offers*. I learned it the hard way but I'm glad that I did. If your business is not growing, then maybe you might be making the same mistake as I was. You may not be making enough offers.

Now here's the big question, how many *offers* did you make this month?

Another huge mistake of mine was overthinking. Like I mentioned earlier, there are people who just like the mindset where they keep looking for that some connection, getting aligned and no taking action. And other people are those who turn up to every event in the city and go through different YouTube videos and make notes to find new strategies. They simply work to find the right strategy however, they do not work on their mindset. Therefore, to succeed, you need to do both.

How does the world view success as?

In my life, my parents, family, and relatives viewed success as studying, getting a degree, getting a job, buying a house, and finally getting married. However, when I walked that path and reached the so-called 'success', I did not feel successful. Even though I had the money that I wanted to make and all the necessities that life demands, I still did not get the feeling of success.

Then I started viewing success from a different perspective. That was when I realized that I was wrong all along and I should never get caught in other people's view of the world ever again. Therefore, I started looking for different alternatives for success. I discovered a lot of paths and one of them was the Business. When I initially started out in the business world, I was told that the business owners are the worst people in the world. That statement then became my belief and I did not want to be associated as a bad person in my life. After a little experience and age, I found out that everybody was not set out to run a business.

I, myself failed 13 businesses in my life. From networking marketing to software companies, etc. I failed in all of them. With time and experience, I learned what didn't work, however I was getting closer day by day. And with every business that I conducted, I got a step closer to the next step.

I realized that every person has opinion about everything. Sitting in a lounge room they can coach Australian cricket team and talk about how they should be playing cricket.

They will give you lectures about how you should be running the business, and how you should be doing your marketing and other things like that, however they have never run a business themselves and currently working for someone else. The best option is to listen and ignore.

How to know who you should be listening to?

I always make sure I listen to the right people. For me, advice of my mentor is the most important advice in the business.

If you want to be the owner of a successful business, then these are the four pillars to success:

- You need to have a quantum mind. Monkey mind is not going to lead you anywhere.
- You need expert mentorship.
- You need a proven recipe.
- And lastly, you need a like-minded community.

With this book, this is what I aim to do. My goal is to give you all four pillars so you can run your business successfully. The question is, what should you be doing to move forward? The first step is to get your foundation right. I really want to ensure that you understand the foundation of the business properly. The second step is to monitor your patterns. Monitor what your world view is. What do you need to change? Who do you need to become? What are the habits that you need or don't need? The third step includes speaking to your potential clients on a daily basis, either directly or indirectly. You are putting offers out there, whether officially or unofficially. You need to start thinking of different ways to reach out to your potential market and make as many offers as possible.

When focusing on how to run your business successfully, one important step is to block external noise. So how do you block the noise? Here are some tips that may help you in blocking out any external noise that may be meddling with your head:

- Stop reading/listening to the NEWS
- Stop wasting time watching TV, scrolling through Facebook feeds, and binge-watching on Netflix
- Replace your Facebook App with the Facebook Page App so you can concentrate only on your business and not any other useless news feed
- Turn off notifications on your phone (except for calls and SMS)
- Stop going to business functions and dinners (with the intention to build your business)
- Start conducting strategy meetings with your potential clients

One important thing to keep in mind is that everything is governed by The Law of Nature, including business. Business is not something unique, everything is a part of the Law of Nature. Therefore, do not fight the market. Most of us make the mistake of fighting the market. Go with the market and flow with the market. This is what will make you rich. Now I am going to talk about my view of the world. As I said earlier, everybody has got their frame that they hold and walk around and use it to see things. So how do I see the world? This is how I see the world:

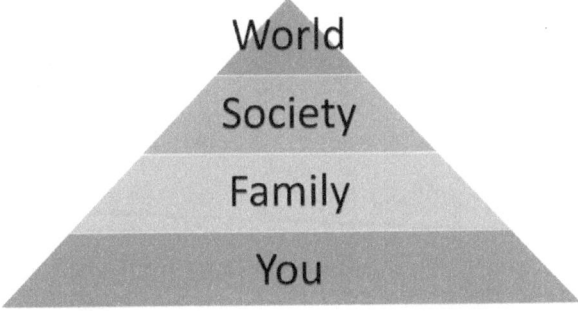

I see this concept really well and I have a belief that everyone is doing their best based on their values and beliefs. But let's not forget that they have acquired these beliefs based on their past experiences, family, society, and the world that they live in.

When somebody comes to me with their problems, I try to understand how they actually see the world. In the same way, your clients also have a view of the world. They view things differently. Their view is based on many factors like the things they like or dislike, their family, their upbringing, etc. Therefore, when someone says something to me, I simply tell myself that is how he sees the world. When I say this to myself, I do not have anger or an opinion, I don't have a perception about that. What I only see is, *"This is how s/he sees the world"*. You should accept their perception about things.

Now here's the golden rule of business. For people to buy from you, *you both must see the world from a single frame.*

By now we are well aware that everyone is trying their best to reach their desired self. Everyone is looking for a way to transport in order to reach their desired future. That transport could be provided by you or by somebody else. They are all looking for it, which is why people are buying services as such.

My mentor told me, you need three things to make any business successful:

- FOWTW – Find Out What They Want
- GAGI – Go and Get It
- GITT – Give It to Them

If you know what the customers want, your business is to give it to them. This is all what a business is about. People usually see the trend and seem to follow it. For example, if a person's dad was an accountant, that person is most likely to end up being an accountant too. And then they wonder, why businesses are not flourishing.

Let's talk about the expert industry now. Expert here I mean, you have acquired certain skillset in last many years and now you are using that skillset to make money. For example: Accountants, Life Coaches, Real Estate Agents, Mortgage Brokers etc. As you know that most people want to get to their desired future quicker & faster. This is when they need expert help. People require expert advice to reach their goals quicker and faster. The expert who helps people in reaching their desired self, quicker and faster makes most of the money. People need your advice in this field because they are unable to do it themselves. If people could do it themselves, they would have done it. But they don't. Why? They need experts who have been doing this for a while now.

These people want results fast. They do not want to go to university and waste their time there and learn how to create a program. They can simply hire somebody to make the program for them. After all my failures, the most important lesson I learned is that I had to start-up all my businesses myself, without anyone's help. This means that I wanted to create a platform and I thought I had the solution to people's problems.

Every time I created a business, my main focus was only me, myself, and I. Everything I did was related to me. I had an accounting degree, therefore, that made me think I ought to have an accounting business. When I had an IT degree, I thought I needed an IT business. I loved coaching people, and so I started a coaching business. As mentioned in the previous chapters, setting up a business requires having an entrepreneur mindset. You do not care what you have done or what business you want. You find out what the market wants. What products does it need to fill the gap in their lives? You need to evaluate if you have the skillset to fulfill this want in the market or do you have to hire someone for it? Richard Branson did not care what he wanted, he cared only for what the market wanted. People think about themselves, whereas the business world thinks about what the market wants in order for it to succeed. If you know more about your target market than they know about themselves, your business will turn out to be a success.

Business owners make the mistake of spending time convincing their clients of a need that they do not have, instead of finding out what do the clients want.

So here is the recipe to success for any business:

- Ask them what they want
- Get clear on that
- Give it to them

Question is, how can you find out what they really want? Simple answer. **ASK**. Ask your clients what they really want. Conduct a market research. Speak to the potential clients and dig out for what they want. Some steps that you can follow are:

- Pick a niche target market
- Understand what they want much better than they would know
- Then create a product to help them fill that gap

So, your advice is going to fill the gap between the current situation and the desired future. How do you deliver your advice? The best way to deliver your advice is:

1. Group sessions,
2. One-on-one sessions,
3. and Online.

Chapter 12
Experts Journey

"An expert is a man who has made all the mistakes which can be made, in a narrow field."

– *Niels Bohr.*

In this chapter, I am going to discuss what is important for your business. Your monkey mind wants to do everything except for what is required and there is a possibility that you may follow your monkey mind too. However, you need to do the work and stick to it.

Each of us gets paid to provide advice. It doesn't matter what you do today, whether you are cleaning the offices or you doing accounting for people, people usually look for advice from you. Anybody can get their work done from somewhere else. But they come to you, why? Because they are looking for expert advice. They are buying your expert advice.

We refer to this as the expert industry because you get paid for your expert advice. All of us are experts in something and we all have certain knowledge for something or the other. This industry is known as the expert industry where people are being paid for their advice.

So how do experts deliver their advice?

- Groups where people come together and listen to you and attend your workshops / events / trainings
- 1-on-1 sessions where you are talking to one client only and are delivering your advice personally
- Done for you - is where you do the work for someone i.e. Accountants get paid to file the tax returns
- Do it with them - In some businesses client and the expert do things together.
- They do it themselves - Online delivery is where you give advice through video programs and your client does all the work.

We all have this clear concept now that we all are moving from our current situation to desired future. This same rule applies to our clients as well. Clients are also moving from their current state to their desired future. The same thing applies to business. In the previous chapters I've mentioned that no matter what it is, we are all meant to grow. The only drawback is that we being business owners stop that growth based on our beliefs and mindset.

As per the law of nature, businesses too have to grow. The law of nature is applicable in every aspect of life. Since we understand that a business needs to grow, all we need to do is provide that environment for businesses to grow. In this chapter, we are going to create an environment in which your business can grow.

I am going to talk about the different steps that you need to take in order to transcend your business to the next level. Businesses have different stages just like humans. From birth till old age, during each stage of life, we humans have different needs and demands. Similarly, different businesses have different needs. We treat our business as if it was pretty same all the time. Same steps, same functions, and everything else at the same time. Everything was pretty much done in the same way. I didn't actually understand it during my early days. During the early days our business is much like a baby. A baby requires a different kind of attention, compare to a teenager. Business is like that as well. When the baby is young, you need to feed, pamper, shower, etc. As the baby grows up, there are some things that he/she is able to do on his/her own.

The same theory applies in the business world as well. Sometimes, when we are starting the business, we need to do certain things in a certain way. In this chapter, I would like to emphasize on those important things such as what you must do in the business, why you need to do those certain things, and why are people failing in doing so? Why are people doing only one or two things and not what is important?

THE FAST GROWTH METHOD

Let me present the step by step process to start with. I will try to explain it as simple as possible. It is not necessary that you should be on the first step to start it. You can be standing at any level and are working to move forward. What I am trying to show is that there are different levels and if you haven't stepped in the business world yet, the following steps are the easiest way to start with.

- Do it for the Client – Anybody can start a service delivery business easily and quickly. This is one of the easiest businesses to start. You provide your clients with services like cleaning or doing their accounts. It is pretty easy for the client as they do not have to do the work.
- Do it with Them – There are certain things that the client does and certain things that you do. You will be doing some of the work with your client and some of the work will be done by the client. For example: You build their website and they provide the copyright material for webpages.
- 1-on-1 – At this level, you work 1-on-1 with the client and provide high touch service. They can ask you questions any time and you help them complete certain tasks.
- Group – When you get better at doing 1-on-1, the next level is groups. When your advice has more value and people recognize that value, they would love to sit down and listen

to you in a group setting. This is because your advice is more valuable.

- Online – It is almost the same as Groups. When your advice becomes valuable, people would love to listen to you online. Some may not be able to come to you as a group or meet you for a 1-on-1 session; therefore, they come online.

One big mistake most people make before they come to me is that they try to sell online programs first without going through the process step by step.

You must know that if you are trying to sell online first before going through the previous steps, it will be very hard. You need a lot of social following, a lot of trust in the market place and huge marketing budget. Before getting into the step no.5, you need to ensure that you have gone through the previous steps.

Here's the big secret, if you are selling $297 item or you are selling $3997 package. The effort to sell either of them is the same.

Experts Journey

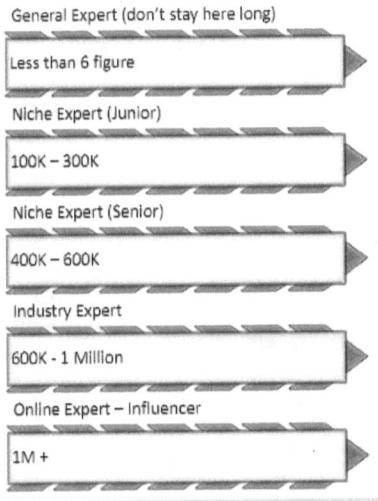

The above figure shows how the expert journey actually looks like. As mentioned above that we all are experts, and this is the journey that we all go through. When we start our journey, we all start as general experts. We are pretty generic.

We speak, generally explaining what we do. For example, one would simply say I'm an IT guy, or an accountant, or a business developer. These people do the work, but they are very generic, which is why they make the least amount of money compared to other experts.

The problem with generic experts is that they are not able to move further in their specific area. Generic is very hard to sell. Why? Because everyone in the market is generic, so they compete with other experts at the same level. The second step in the above figure is when people get better at their business, they become Junior Niche Experts. People become niche experts who are very specific toward the niche, such as, they only work with real estate agents, or corporate people, or life coaches, etc.

As people progress, they become experts in very specific niche markets. When they become a niche expert, people know them in that space. This is the stage when the business can run on autopilot. It all depends on where you are in this cycle. Many people wonder whether they can cater to more than one market. Yes, you can as long as you start with one specific niche at a time. Start small and then gradually increase it.

If you take a look at the biggest influencers of this industry out there, do they serve everybody? Yes, they do. But they haven't started it that way. For example, Tony Robbins only started with health. He only helped people with their health in the beginning. Then gradually, he expanded to relationships and so on. Currently, for the past ten years, he has expanded to business as well. Therefore, he expanded his niche market to different areas and so now, he caters almost all aspects. That is why you need to be really specific when catering a niche. Once you have successfully captured that niche, then you can expand to something new. For example, if you are looking to work in real estate, you don't just want to be a generic real estate agent. Start with focusing on one specific niche. You can focus only on people who want to buy their first property. Then you can move forward to catering other niche markets within the property industry.

I would like to give you an example of a Facebook friend name Ian Ugarte. He runs a company called "Small is the new big". He is a perfect example of niche expert. He didn't compete in the entire property market like most do. He picked up a very small niche market, helping investors create 'share housing' which he calls high income real estate system.

Now looking back at the steps of the business process, which is, do you think has the biggest limitation? One of the biggest limitations in *"Do it for the Client"* model is that you are person who is serving (delivering) your clients; you are also the person who is blocking the flow. This means that your business cannot expand because you are in the middle. You can only cater to a certain number of clients and are not able to do more than after a certain number.

The last step of the expert's journey is to become an online expert. You know those people who live a life sitting on the beach and are selling online courses; that is the last step. You have to go through the step by step process to reach that level. There are no shortcuts to success. People think that they can skip other steps and do one to succeed. That is where they are wrong.

You need to go through all the steps, so people will know you gradually, and then they are able to trust you. Once they are able to trust you, it becomes a lot easier to sell it to them.

Now, moving deeper into the expert's journey, you must create different levels of packages / services you offer based on your client's journey. For example, if you are running an accounting firm, you may know that in an accounting firm when somebody comes to you for the first time, they have certain requirements. And when you fulfill those requirements, the same client moves to level 2 and now have different set of requirements. What you must do is understand client's journey and create different offers in your business to help the same client on different levels. Such as in level 1, you are working generically with everybody.

In level 2, you work with a very specific number of people. The fun part is, you give the same advice to people of different levels; however, the delivery model is very different. I suggest to have at least 3 levels in your business to help your client on 3 different level of requirements.

What is your Step One?

Your first step is to pick a niche market. You need to decide what your niche market is. In other words, who do you serve? The end goal is to become the go-to person of your niche market so that when your potential client thinks of that problem, they think of your name.

Experts Trap

Let's get into the real stuff now. The big problem is that the experts' businesses are started by employees. This means that, when an employee becomes tired of his 9 to 5 job, s/he believes that s/he can do the same thing much better by starting her/his own business. The employee thinks that because of him/her, his/her employer's business is running. Nonetheless, they forget one main thing. Delivery is the last step of the customer sales cycle (not the first one). Employees forget that there are other departments of the business that are working too and he/she is unaware of the work done within the other departments.

The biggest mistake that employees make is that they get into many fields like technology, sales, Google Ads, Facebook Marketing of which they have no knowledge about. They get involved in all the operations of the business that are not important in the initial stages of business. Why? Because they believe that they need technology or certain tools to help their businesses succeed.

Experts Trap - I need certain tools / gadgets to make my business successful

To make any business successful, these are the typical steps that one has to take:

1. Find out who do you want to serve
2. Their current situation and desired future
3. Discover the gap
4. Create an offer based on the gap to act as a vehicle
5. Conduct strategy session and start making offers

But what happens is that they get involved in stuff like websites, social media, logo, business cards, etc. without even having a client yet. They believe that these are the things that matter when running a business. I was someone who used to believe in that too. What you should be doing instead is spending all your energy in getting clients.

Then I realized that I should have people who will pay me before I get myself to do the other stuff. You must be thinking that these things are important too (and they are). But not in the beginning. At least until you have 5-10 clients. Don't get caught up in the employee mindset. You need to get the clients first and create your market before marketing it and branding it elsewhere. Nobody really cares about your logo or your website.

The reason I failed in my businesses is that I worked extra hard to get all those tools. I thought that if a client comes and if I do not have all those tools, my company will not seem legit and the client will not give me the business. However, today, my view of the world is that I need to get a client to pay me and get the money rolling before I get into the other tools and tech.

Why do we get caught into the expert's trap? Because of FOMO (Fear Of Missing Out). This is the biggest issue. People believe that they are going to miss out if they do not have all the necessary tools for a business, and so they believe that they will not be following the trend. It took me a while to understand that you have a plan and take that plan step by step.

One tip that I need to give you here is, start making calls to book strategy meetings. When you start a business, the most important thing is getting clients. In order to get clients, you need to have meetings and phone calls. (more details on this topic also available later in the book) Without them, you do not have a client, and without a client, you do not have a business. You have to do the work in order to get your business up and running and the work is having strategy meetings with your potential clients. The voice in your head will distract you doing other things i.e. setup website, create logo, organize emails etc.

Don't get distracted by the other voices. You need to take the responsibility as you are the one owning the business. You are the person who is building something from scratch. You need to be disciplined enough to stop yourself from listening to those voices. I would suggest that your first focus must be having strategy meetings with your potential clients.

Different Types of Markets

There are three types of markets, and you need to think and select the market that you are planning to play in. The three markets are:

- Health Market
- Wealth Market
- Relationship Market

Each of these markets has submarkets. The mistake that people make is competing in the main markets instead finding their blue ocean submarkets. People will go and open the same business that is present in the market and compete in that market. According to the book *"Blue Ocean Strategy,"* everybody competes in the market that has been flooded by people or other businesses, and this area is called the *"Red Ocean."* You need to look for a market in the space known as the *"Blue Ocean"* because there are no sharks in the blue ocean, so it is easy to work it out there. For example, when TV and radio came out, we forced people to buy products by spraying and praying. However, when the internet emerged, it opened up small niche markets. People have written books about *"How to Train Your German Shepherd."* This is a very specific niche market and a very small market, but if you count the number of people around the globe who are interested in such a market, it equals to a lot of people.

Let's take an example of the health industry. You will see a lot of ads that say *"Lose 10kg in 90 days by attending our boot camp"*. However, if you try and compete differently in the submarkets, you can place an ad that says, *"Lose 10 kg using our Keto Diet without going to the gym"*. This is called Blue Ocean Strategy. This type of headline must be focused on what your ideal client wants the most and what they dislike the most in order to create your own unique marketing headline. Such as in this case, people want to lose weight, but they dislike going to the gym.

In this example Keto diet is a blue ocean strategy targeting very specifically those who hate going to the gym but still want to lose weight.

Chapter 13
Target Market

"Identify your niche and dominate it. And when I say dominate, I just mean work harder than anyone else could possibly work at it."

- Nate Parker

In the previous chapter, we discussed that you must have a niche market. You do not want to be a generic person. When you are generic, you make less money while serving everybody else. Therefore, I suggest that you target specific niches. *Money is in niches*

In order to target the niche, you must start generically. But then, as you move forward, you need to specialize in a niche. Once you have captured that niche, you can move forward to another niche. You need to be an expert in that niche. People should know you in that specific market, and then you can move forward to the next level.

If you remember the *"Value Ladder"* from chapter 8, there was a portion of the top that is the *"imagination."* This area refers to the people who use their minds to make money. In today's society, people who are on top do not copy anyone else. They are the ones who create their own rules. They are the ones who invent. They look at the market as an observer.

We all start with modeling someone's work, then we innovate and invent.

They analyze the market and then create their own rules. They understand the fact that everyone has their own view of the world.

Society's Current Paradigm

Our world says that you must have a general knowledge. It is a common belief that if you do not know the capital of the USA or where Uluru is, then you are not an educated person. The society makes you feel bad for not knowing these facts. This is where people try to get information only to fill that gap because they feel that they need to have general knowledge. However, in the business world, the generic rule does not apply.

In business, you are paid the most when you are specialized, or you have the authority in that special domain. Therefore, you need to be in a position of authority, and you need to specialize in a specific niche. Let's take the example of GPs. GPs don't get paid well. (compare to specialists) Why? Because they are general practice doctors. Comparatively, ENT specialists are paid heaps of money. Why? Because they have specialized in one specific niche.

If I reflect back on my life, I have changed so many careers. I started my career as a programmer. Then I became a manager, which is a completely different take on the career. Later on, I became an IT architect and then a business owner. I did my bachelor's in accounting, but I never worked in that field. Even though I had different niches and domains, I changed accordingly. Therefore, you do not have to stick to one niche. But your goal must be to become the go-to person of the niche market.

Now if you look at the market today, most businesses have defined their niche market but are still not making money. When you know who you want to serve, and you have the product, yet no one is buying Why? Because they skip the last step. The last step is to solve a very *specific problem within that niche market*. You cannot solve every problem that arises in your niche.

Society's View of the World

Let's talk about business patterns. If we talk about society, it includes all the things that we have mentioned earlier, such as values and beliefs that you got from your friends and family and your surroundings. The same theory is applied to business as well. Most businesses look and feel the same. So what people do is that they look at other people. For example, if I am a masseuse, I try to look at what other masseuses are doing. When doing that, there are two things involved.

One, looking from a perspective of observation regarding how it works. The other thing is, seeing everything from their view of the world and believe what they see. This is what most people do. They don't understand things; they just follow through and become a part of their view of the world. They setup their business exactly same way as the other business in the market. That's why most businesses look and feel the same in the marketplace.

This is why most businesses have the same business message, marketing methods, almost the same websites, and even the same sales funnels. The question is, how do you get out of this situation? To begin with, you need to become an observer. The observer asks the questions and does not believe in the lies and the society's view of the world. The observer looks at everything around. He observes his competition, the marketing, and what people are doing today. You become that observer and you start asking the question, *"Why are they doing this?"* We business owners are educated and smart people. We can understand the fact that different businesses have different ways to make their sale. It is not necessary that the ways they adopt will work for you too.

Why People Hire You?

People have a current state and they have a future that they desire. Every person in this world wakes up in the morning and works toward achieving their desired future. That is the reason as to why people hire you. They need somebody's help to fill that gap at a short period of time.

Everyone out there has different needs, values, and beliefs. If you do not pick a specific target market, it becomes really hard to tell where these specific people are going. Everybody is going somewhere, however if you are not aware of where they are going, it becomes really hard to design a program/service/product. If you do not pick one problem within a specific niche, you begin solving too many problems.

This leads to your clients getting confused. That is why you need to pick a niche and pick a specific problem within that niche.

Here's a secret of Business Success

As I've mentioned time and time again, everything is governed by the Law of Nature. Business is no exception to this law. When I claimed that your clients have their dreams and desires, what I mean is that they want to go from one place to the other. They also have the desired future.

Traditional View of the Target Market

Traditional market states that my target market is static i.e. accountants, coaches, or dentists, etc. However, there is a big flaw in that. Like mentioned that all of us are moving toward a desired future, then does that mean that your target market is also moving towards their desired future? Yes, your target market is also moving, they are going from their current state to the desired future. Meaning, your target market is NOT static.

People may believe that their clients are accountants, but what they don't understand is that their clients, whether accountants or not, are going somewhere. The question is where are they going? What are they becoming? That is why I advise that you need to target a specific market because you can easily find it out by simply asking them, *"Where are they now and where they want to be?"*

When you meet certain people and speak to certain people, that's when you understand them. Some people want to become coaches, some people want to stop smoking, some people want to make more money, and some people want to have more clients. Everybody is going somewhere. Everybody wants to become something. Honestly speaking, we don't care where they are today. We are more interested in where they are going. If you are the person who knows where they are going, you can take them to their destination. The old view of the target market is static. Businesses would only cater to accountants, or to marketing companies. The new view of the target market is that your target market is going somewhere, the question is, where?

Here's another one, when you ask a business owner who do they serve, they usually respond by saying that they are a B2B business, or they are a B2C business. If we look at a business through a human's perspective, then who is running the business? I truly believe that there is no B2B or B2C businesses, we all are P2P businesses; People to People business.

New View of The Target Market

My new view of the world is, if you want a successful business, you need to keep in mind that your target market is moving somewhere (not static). Your target market has a destination and they are working on it every day to reach their desired place. Your job is to find out where they are going. Once you do that, you can easily take them to their destination.

You may believe that they are going somewhere you want to go but just to make sure, ask them. This information is helpful when you are creating a product or a service for your clients. I interviewed more than 40+ business owners. All of them told me one similar problem. The biggest problem they faced was that they didn't know how to scale their business. They were not aware of how to consistently get new clients. I truly believe that if you don't know how to get a client or getting clients because the business fundamentals are not clear. Once those fundamentals are clear, operating a business becomes easy. If you have a solution to their problems and you know where your clients are going, you can simply offer to take them there. In the previous chapter, I explained the expert's trap. The expert's trap states that the reason most businesses fail is because they are started by employees and as an employee mindset people believe they must have certain tools to make business successful. In this chapter, I will explain how to come out of that expert's trap and what to focus on to be successful in your business.

I'm going to define the attributes of a business. Just like a body requires certain parts such as the heart, liver, brain, etc., just like that each of these parts have to work together in order to make the body function properly. Businesses work in the same way. There is no exception in this case, as when you provide the environment to the business, it is meant to grow. In order for a business to succeed, you require 4 types of people in your business.

First, we need *visionaries* (*entrepreneurs*).

Visionaries are the people who have a vision about the business. These are the people who know and understand where the business is going. They are the people who talk about the high-level stuff. The second person is the *manager*. The manager is the person who manages business operations in the business.

He is the one who optimizes the system and creates the system. The third person is the *leader*. He is the ones who manage the artists. The fourth type of person is the *artist*. They are those who design the products. They are the ones who deliver the solution. They are the ones who perform the work.

One of the biggest issues that we face in the world today is that most of the people are coming out to be engineers or artists. The engineers and artists work to make the product look good. Becoming a business owner and becoming an artist are two different things. If you are becoming a business owner, then you need to know that you have to be a business owner and concentrate on all 4 roles (not just one)

Your Business Identity

Who are you in your business? Are you the visionary, the manager, the leader or are you the artist? You need to identify who you are in your business because when you are clear about who you are, you can get other people to help you.

THE FAST GROWTH METHOD

After a lot of contemplation, I concluded that I will be the ***visionary*** for my business. Why? Because I used to be an artist. I used to be the guy who was busy designing the software. I was the one doing the work at the backend. Therefore, I decided not to be that guy in my business. So I decided to hire team members to fill the other three roles.

In my business, I hired a developer (artist), manager & a leader to help me out. This is important for all of us and we have to understand who we really are in our business. Today, if you do not have the resources to hire people, you should not feel bad. You might be the person who is playing all the 4 roles in your business. That only means that you will be wearing a different hat at different times when required.

This does not mean that you should ignore the rest of the roles and focus only on one role. When I realized that I was a visionary. I could see things in a bigger picture. I could actually put things together really nicely, create models and designs. The only thing I lacked was the skill set of being a manager, a leader, and an engineer. I went and spoke to a couple of people on my previous team and convinced them to work with me in my business and to my luck, they all said yes!

One of the team members was a project manager and I asked him whether he was willing to be the GM of my company. He agreed. I hired him to manage the operations of my company. Then we went on to hire a number of engineers who were responsible to do the backend work.

This does not mean that I did not take responsibility of those areas. I had given every person their responsibility while I came up with the visions of the company. One important thing that everyone has to do is to find out their dominant side. What do you actually want to do? What do you like doing? Some of you may enjoy delivering the work and working on the craft. There is no good and bad to it. If you really like doing it, then you like doing it. There are a lot of other people willing to do the remaining work. You need to find out what role are you going to play in your business. Once you have that cleared out, you can hire other people to do the other roles. However, you need to keep in mind that all four roles are equally important when running a business. But in certain situations, certain roles are more important than the others.

As most businesses are started by employees, what is their first priority? Their first priority is to make the product look the best and to improve their skill sets. They believe that by improving the skill sets, they will be able to improve their businesses. Nevertheless, you need to look at the other sides as well.

Your job is to find out what is your dominant business identity? What are your responsibilities in your business? What role are you playing in your business? Are you an entrepreneur? Are you the manager? Are you the leader? Or are you the artist? Identify your role so that you are aware of what role you need to play and whether you are ignoring any other roles. Lastly, let others carry out the rest of the roles. If you are an entrepreneur, then you need to stop worrying about creating a website, bookkeeping, and other detail-oriented tasks. Let the role players play their own roles!

Chapter 14
Transformation

"The real transformation is when your clients get their desired results, everything else is just a filler"

– **Jag Jassel**

In this chapter, we will talk more about target market along with discussing the message to market and your offer to your target market. Also, we will talk about how most people believe they will get success by luck and that adding more value means they will make more money. You should always remember that success does not come overnight.

You have to work hard for it. After studying so many successful people, after going through so many books, after applying those principles in my business and others' businesses as well, I realized business is just simple mathematics. For example, you get A+B = C and when we put them together, we get the results.

We get the recipe and when we put those ingredients required, we're going to get a baked cake at the end. If Jamie Oliver comes here, provides you with the recipe and asks you to bake a cake, chances are that you will get a cake exactly like the one you would find at a 5-star hotel. People will believe that because Jamie Oliver told us. But if a random person says this to us, we won't trust him. It's because people don't have that trust and faith in everyone. Sometimes, people don't believe in themselves as well. So by the end of this, I need you to have that belief, have that faith that you are going to take your business to the next level. I am here to show you the strategies, to show you the math, to show you those missing pieces and variables which actually create the business when put together. That's what we are going to do. You have to believe in these steps; luck will come when you are working in the right direction. Luck will be in your favor a hundred percent when you know what you want. When you don't know what you want, luck cannot do anything.

So, let's talk about what most people believe in. We have already discussed the value ladder in chapter 8 but what actually is this value and how do we get the value? Let's take a step back and see what most people do in a business environment. For example, if I want to give more value, I just need to add more stuff in the basket.

Similarly, if I want to add more value to people's lives, I'll do that by giving more services (stuff). If I spent 30 minutes with them and that's the amount of time I invest, I have to spend 40 minutes or 2hrs. I have to spend more or give them more stuff and that's what most people believe. That's the normal way of looking at more value in business. However, that is just a myth and I can tell you that it doesn't help.

So what matters the most in the business game? What matters the most is your *clients' results*. Everything else around that is just a filler. The reason people hire you because they want results. They have a current situation, they have a desired future and they have a gap, which they want to fill. They hire people like you to fill that gap quicker and faster. So it doesn't really matter how much time you spend or how educated you are or how many degrees you hold. Nobody cares! Especially your clients. **They only care about their results, nothing else.**

Transformation

The next thing that comes is what transformation you can bring to your clients world? How can you fill that gap quicker and faster? The price should be based on the value, not the time you spend. It should be based on the transformation you bring to them.

There are certain steps that you need to take in order to bring transformation and make your product different.

- So the first step is to find out what your client's desired future is. Where are they heading and what do they actually want?

- What services you can offer to help them get there in a short period of time.

- You should identify what's costing your clients to stay back where they already are. Is it costing them their health? Their freedom? Or their relationship? It can be anything, and it's your job to find that out.

- What value will your service add once they achieve their desired future? Would you help them improve their relationship(s)? Would you be able to put them at ease? It is the most important step as in this step, you realize what you are giving them back.

After you know what exactly your client wants, help them achieve it quickly with the help of your product or service.

Pricing

How do you price it? As I said earlier, pricing is not based on the hours. Never think about how much time it will take for you to create a logo, you need to look at what's costing your client to stay there. Some people could be struggling with their health or with their business, there is always something people are struggling with.

Now ask yourselves, can you help them with their struggles? What value your service can add to their lives? What products can you offer? How frequently will you able to offer the products to them?

This is what happens when a person enters the world of business for the first time. Their mindset is that they are going to go out there in hustle mode and get a client for themselves. Every month, they are in hustle mode. Eventually, they get tired as it is not a long-term strategy to grow a business.

One of the biggest problems behind the failure of most businesses is because they don't have a consistent income. They don't even know how much money they are going to make the next month. However, if they are working for someone else, they know they are going to earn a specific amount next month because they are working as an employee.

You don't need to plan much. If you want to grow your business, the very first thing that you really need is a consistent income. How do you get that consistent income? By having the consistency of getting something done for your clients on weekly, fortnightly or monthly basis. Now you need to decide regarding the service we talked about previously; how can you provide that service to different levels of requirements for your clients?

The biggest question you must answer for getting consistent revenue is – what service you can render on weekly, fortnightly or monthly basis to help your clients move forward?

How do you set a price when offering your service or product? If you remember, I have different steps done for you and while following those steps, you develop your levels of service simultaneously. In the first step, you are doing everything for your client. Somebody comes to you, they want to get something fixed and you have a solution for their problem with a price. Remember it is the price for the value, not for the number of hours you spent.

For example, our company charges $2000 monthly looking after the business owners.

- We provide coaching services to coaches / consultants. It's a 12-month program called **Champions Club**, helping coaches and consultants reach 50k to 100K per month revenue.

This is a perfect example and we will talk about it in detail later. For your customer, you are not just someone who provides them with a service or a product. Fact is, when you get into a business deal with your customer, you are basically taking them on a journey. Once the customer enters the premises of your business, then that's where the journey begins. They don't know anything about your business, they just have a problem and you are responsible to provide them with a solution. Remember when you help them get what they want, it doesn't mean they do not have a new desired future after that. Everyone is continuously moving, heading somewhere.

We, in terms of business, are also going in some direction, therefore we have to take control of where we are heading. We have to draw a line and tell ourselves, *this is where I begin, this is my gate from where people can enter through the journey with me.* The way it works in our company is to help business owners with 90 days Fast Growth Program.

We teach them how they can take their business to the next level in 90 days. This is our entry gate and we provide them this service in one package, however they have a longer journey after that. At each step, the needs of the customers change and we have different products available in our business to cater for each step for the same niche market.

Coaching Industry

Hoping by now you have a niche market that you work (or going to work) with. Now the next step is to find out their current situation and their desired future. Once you have the answers to these three questions, i.e. your niche, current situation, and desired future. The next step is to deliver your solution by providing them your advice. Figure out the steps on how you are going to take them to the desired future in the next 6 to 12 weeks. In this example you are not giving them anything but just your advice. (that's called coaching) The reason I say 6 to 12 weeks is because anything more than that is just way too much.

Whatever program you are running, whether it is 1-on-1 coaching or a group programs, you have to get them some quick results within 3 months. If you don't get them some very quick wins they will get distracted and the negative feedback loop may start which won't be in your favor.

The next question is why would they join your program? They are not joining your program to feel happy. You have to find the real problem and desired future. Sometimes we believe that the way we see the world, other people exactly see it the same way, which is not true. We should always know what is costing our client to stay where they are.

Now after going through the above 6 to 12 week process, what value do you think you have added? Did you help them reach their destination? This is very crucial part of any business success. Most people fail in this section because they deliver the content based on their assumptions. Here's my suggestion, when you onboard any client, you must ask them this question. What are the three things you MUST learn from this program which will make it worth your time and money? And your ONLY job is to deliver what they requested. Sometimes client request some fluff as well i.e. I want to make million dollars in next 3 months or my favorite I want to have 20 new clients (but in reality, they never had one client) so you just want to make sure you don't set unrealistic expectations. You must be very clear on what you can deliver for a client.

I believe the cost for 6 to 12-week program should be somewhere around $2,000 to $10,000 initially. If you have experience of a 10 years+, you know your market really well. You know exactly what your client is willing to pay for your services. You may be able to charge more for this.

Credibility

For people to buy from you, they must find you credible. So, build credibility; that's how people are going to pay you for your advice. Initially, you build that credibility by doing it for someone else (Done For You Service). One of the biggest mistakes I have seen beginners make is that they charge by the hour. You must never charge on an hourly basis. This is a very wrong mindset, it only goes to show that you don't care about the client rather your main concern is the amount of money that you earn. Whenever someone asks me what I charge, I never tell them a standard price. I never talk about the price, I ask them if my service can actually help them with their problem. You need to start selling solutions at first. Everything else is secondary.

THE FAST GROWTH METHOD

The above image is the visual representation of what we just talked about. No matter who you speak to, even if it's the President, everybody has this gap. To fill that gap, there has to be an offer, a product or a service. The following is the game changing information. Now you know your niche market and the results they are looking to achieve. So, when you create your offer, your client and their results are always static. The only variable in this process is your OFFER.

The only thing which will change with time is your offer. You can offer different products / services to the same niche as you know their problems and results they are after. In other words, the target market remains the same, their results remain constant but the only variable that changes is the offer. I am going to give you our example. Our niche market is coaches and consultants. My first offer to my target market was 'build your 7-figure business.' Unfortunately, only 10 people bought our 12-week offer. Then I tried the second offer which was 'Become Micro Industry Celebrity'. We tested the offer in a couple of workshops but it didn't work either.

That's where the third offer came in. 'Build your personal brand'. Few people liked this offer. A lot of people came to the workshop but again only few bought the next step. So we tried a few other things along the way. The only variable that's constantly changing is the offer in order to identify what people actually like. In the end, I came up with this 'Learn how to generate more leads for your business without spending more on advertisement'. This was my last offer and this is where I am today. We have tried it four to five times. It worked for us and a lot of people came in. In the next six months, I may have different offer.

Even though we run a big coaching company but I don't go crazy after advertisement, I don't spend a significant amount on it to begin with, instead I test my offer on 4 to 5 people. I start with just $200. If it works, I go ahead and increase the amount to $5000 per month and so on. I know it works, I know people will buy it. Therefore, there is a system which will help in generating income. I am a big believer in offers and systems. Don't guess or play the game in your head. There is a process for you to understand your business. I could have just sat idly and thought about what I am going to do but I chose to test my market instead. I didn't stand at the sideline, I actually played the game. What I have learnt is that most people just think too much and do not take any actions. Thinking doesn't help in this case, what helps is going out and actually testing it. Do not spend too much time thinking and mind mapping.

I remember at my one of the earlier workshops, I met a girl. Let's call her Julie. Julie came to meet me at backstage and she was super excited about establishing her own business. Just watching her excited filled me with excitement too. After a year and a half, I got connected with her again at an event. I met her and asked her what happened to her business.

I really wanted to know because I still remember how excited she was about it. I already assumed her business was going to make a million dollars or more within the span of two years. When I asked how her business was going, she replied, *"I am still deciding the name for my business,"* and I was like *"What? For a year and a half, you've been deciding the name of the business?"*

She said, *"Yeah, I've been busy with a couple of other things, I am going to decide it quickly and start very soon"*. I was astonished at what she told me. It was unbelievable. So take my advice, and don't be Julie! And spend most of your precious time in thinking back and forth about just one thing. Go ahead and take the jump, test the market and see the wonders you will experience. One advice I can give you going forward is that you don't change your niche market and since you know what they want, therefore you just have to get to give a tempting offer to your clients.

Things take time, and if your first offer isn't as appealing to your target market as you thought it would be, don't feel let down. You will learn from trial and error, and eventually, there will come a point where you will give them an offer which they will accept without a second thought.

What most people do is that they try one or two offers to their niche market and if they don't work, they just completely change the entire niche market. This is a huge mistake because now you are starting from the beginning. Nevertheless, it's important to know your niche market and their problems (the gap in their lives) and craft the offer which best suits their needs.

How to Communicate Your Offer?

The next step is how you deliver your message to the market. At first, my message to the market was really ineffective. I didn't understand this concept, it was like I was talking to my target market but they didn't even know what I was saying. It felt like I was speaking a different language. Conveying a clear message to the market is very critical. Most businesses don't have a clear message, and some of them are just shouting. That's what most people are doing on social media today; clients don't understand and they get pissed instead, just because they are speaking a totally different language than that of their customers'.

Another reason is that most don't talk about the problems their potential client is facing instead they only talk about themselves. A clear, precise, and spot-on message is very powerful. Once you get it right, you don't have to shout. You don't need Facebook posts or blogs or any other social media platform for that matter. People will be happy to pay for your services if your message is clear to them.

What is a good message to the market?

Product

Solution To Problem

In the above picture, on the left frame, there is a tap of water running. Water is available for free in our country. You don't need to pay for it. Water is a product. Now in shopping centers, people sell these bottled water from $2 to $4, depending on the brand you are buying. So my question is, for something that is available for free, why do people pay $4 for it. The answer is because this bottled water is not just water but a solution to a problem. People pay for solutions, not for the product.

What's the lesson here for people who just sell products? If you are focusing on making your product better, you can be beaten by your competitors easily.

Another example of this would be, *"Name a burger joint?"* The first thing that pops in your mind would be McDonald's, however ask yourself if their products are the best in the market? There are people who would say if you eat McDonald's you are just one step closer to your death bed, yet McDonald's is still the number one brand in the world. People still pay for its products. Why? Because they don't care about the product, they care about the solution. Sell solutions to the people, not the products.

Another important thing is what does the market actually want? How do we ask them what they want? For that, we have to conduct market research. Create a Google form for your business and start asking questions like:

- What is your #1 challenge?
- What's your desired GOAL this year?

- If you could have a magic wand, what would you wish?
- What do you aspire to be, do or have?
- On a scale of 1-10, how motivated are you to get that?
- What frustrates you?
- What's most important to you?
- What you believe your unique ability is?
- What worries you?

Create this survey form and send it to people regardless if they were your previous clients or similar people in the niche market. Send it to at least 30 people. The questions above are just examples. You got to have your own questions, make sure the questionnaire isn't too long.

It's high time that you stop thinking and start asking. Every market and every person has a gap. Nobody is perfect. You just need to go out there and find it.

Remember the rule of ONE

- *One Target Market*
- *One Problem*
- *One Solution*

Chapter 15
Sales in Business

"Become the person who would attract the results you seek."

-Jim Cathcart

We have talked a lot about how important it is to choose a specific niche market and stick to it. In regards to that, people have asked me why we need to have just one niche market. People are interested in serving many people and not just a limited circle of people. The way that the business works is not all over the place. Business does not grow when scattered. You will end up being confused and confusing those who are associated with you and your business.

The reason that Henry Ford was really famous is not that he built a car. Cars were built even before he made one. In fact, Henry Ford was famous because he did one of the famous things in the modern industrial age. He created the manufacturing system. He created the system of the conveyer belt where you do not have to move the people, but you move the car parts. He created that platform where car parts could easily move to get to different places. Business is exactly the same.

For example, if you are running a business, you have different niche markets. The niche markets could be life coaches, real estate agents, yoga instructors, mortgage brokers, etc. What you are currently doing is that you are creating material for each niche market that you cater to. Each time that you go and speak to a mortgage broker, or a yoga instructor, or a real estate agent, you realize that they are very different people. However, when you work with one single industry, you meet a very specific type of people. You begin to understand their problem, and you add value. Therefore, I would recommend that you go as narrow as possible when working with a niche. Do not expand it to different levels and different businesses. If you do plan on doing so, you can start expanding within that specific niche. For example, if you are catering to local mortgage brokers, then you may want to expand to national mortgage brokers after them. By doing so, you do not have to create a completely new system. You simply have to enhance the present system. This saves the time that you will need to create an entirely new system.

Sales

Making sales is not easy, and I have learned that the hard way. In this chapter, I would like to focus more on some of the fundamentals of sales. Many people are getting sales wrong, and I am really surprised. I believe that it is mostly because of society's view of the world. The way society sees things and the way that people see things, which is why not everybody is a sales champion.

So let's begin with the current paradigm of the sales world. One of the major beliefs is that making sales is a tedious task. In our society most grow up in a surrounding where everyone perceives sales to be a bad thing. Whoever was making the sales was a bad person, whoever listened to the salespeople were also bad people. In conclusion, making sales is a bad thing. As a result, unconsciously, we start believing those thoughts, whether or not we like it. Another belief of people is that salespeople are bloodsuckers. Whenever they talk to any salesperson, they automatically think, why sales? One more belief includes that traditional salespeople are like old car salespeople who are very pushy.

Now let me try something new. Next time you have your Sales meeting (or Strategy meeting), replace the word *"Sales meeting"* to *"Diagnosis meeting."* Let's take the example of a Doctor. They get a lot of samples on a daily basis. As new medicines come in the market, Doctors get a sample of them. Every time a new medicine is launched, salespeople of the medical company distribute medicines to different clinics and hospitals.

Whenever the doctor gets a new medicine, he does not try to sell those medicines to his patients. In fact, he does not even talk about those medicines. He talks about the patient and his problems. This is the difference between the sales meeting and a diagnosis meeting. Your job is to diagnose the problems with your clients.

One thing you must understand is, when you can't solve their problems or have a solution for their problem, you are kind enough to let them know and refer them to someone else who can help them. Once you do this, your image reaches a different level.

Now replace the concept of sales meeting from your mind and become a person who diagnoses. Let me share an interesting story. I was one of those people who could do everything in my business except sales. I loved to hire people to make sales for me. I tried doing sales myself, but I failed. The reason is that I never understood the concept of sales and in return, I hired bad salespeople. I had a bad experience because it was my responsibility being the owner of the company to understand those fundamentals. I couldn't get people to make the sales when I myself did not know how to do it.

I used to think that people were born to make sales. I had this belief that if a person could talk well, dress well and present himself well, he was a salesperson. I was not capable of being a salesperson because I did not do any of the things above. I came to realize that I could not be a salesperson because they are very aggressive and I am not an aggressive person. Therefore, I do not qualify to be a salesperson. Another belief I had in mind in regards to sales was that it was solely about follow-ups.

Only those people who do not understand the concept of sales talk about follow-ups. When you walk into a clinic, and the doctor diagnoses the problem and gives you the solution, but you respond by saying you will come next week for the solution. Is this possible? No. You would never do that. People look for solutions, and they will grab it whenever they get the chance to. If people are looking for solutions and you are unable to provide them with it, it means that you haven't been able to make your diagnosis properly. Therefore, diagnosis is the number one rule. I also used to think that sales are for those whose first language is English. As I've mentioned, I always had issues with the English language, so I ultimately thought that I could not make sales. However, after doing so many sales calls and speaking to many people during my career, I don't have a fear of sales anymore.

You MUST understand that sales are mandatory for every business. If you have been avoiding to deal with sales, it is because there is something within your mindset that is not accepting the word "sales." My mind was programmed the same way. For me, salespeople were never good. Therefore, it all depends on how you think about sales. It is important to get your mindset right because if don't change your perception about sales, things will just get hard. Sales are the first thing you will need in any business, and if there are no sales, you don't have a business. Instead of considering hiring somebody else, you have to take the initiative to make sales before you put the systems together for someone else to follow. As a business owner and as an entrepreneur, it is your responsibility to make the sales before you go and hire somebody else to do it.

Businesses die because of a lack of sales skills. This is the one skill set that is the most important for a business. If you are not good at sales today, you just need to learn it.

New World View

This is my new way of looking at things. I have changed the old way of looking at sales, and what I look at myself is that I am working to becoming the best salesperson for my business. As I mentioned earlier, if you have some blockage or you think a certain way about sales, it is nothing more than your view of the world. If you are an entrepreneur, making sales is a must.

Client Acquisition Strategy

Client Acquisition Strategy is nothing but tactics to acquire clients for your business. So how do you acquire clients for your business? What is the process you can use for people to walk into your business? I am going to explain the process of how we acquire clients for our business and for our clients. You can take this as an example to create your own strategy for your business.

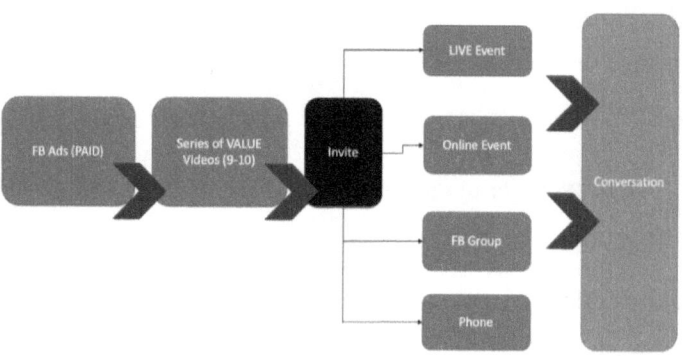

We start with Facebook Ads. These are paid Facebook Ads, which lead people to a series of Value Videos. These are the videos that explain why we do what we do, what do we do, and how we do it. I usually have 8 to 9 videos like that, and I call it "Perception Marketing." After that, we invite viewers to an event, or we ask them to join a Facebook group, or we ask them to have a strategy call. They attend the workshops and the online training sessions, and then we proceed with the process of carrying out a conversation.

This is an end-to-end process for us to acquire a client. You cannot just believe that somebody will come out of nowhere and will become your client. You will not get a client unless you have a process. In our business, I call this entire process, the client acquisition system!

Agitation

Let me explain the behind the scenes of the above process.

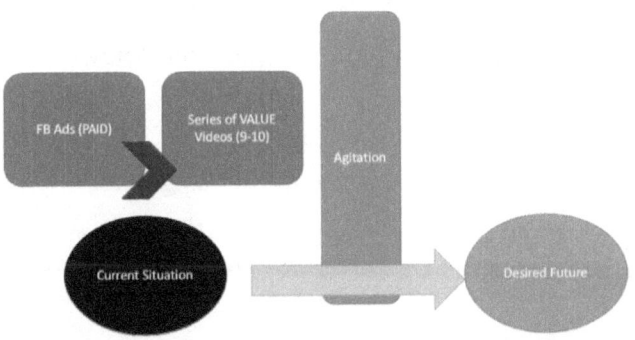

When you show ads and videos to your perfect niche market, your client sees those videos. In this scenario, what you have done is you have made them agitated about the future state. You have practically shown them something that they can get. You showed them their desired future. When the clients are agitated, and you make them an offer, people find ways to get rid of the agitation. They are interested in finding out how they are able to solve their problems and to reach their desired future.

Your job here is to keep your clients agitated. When you provide your agitated clients with the solution to their problems, they will do anything to get rid of that agitation. They will move mountains to get that solution from you as it made them agitated and curious about the desired future, which they never had previously. As a salesperson, you have two jobs. One is highlighting the gap, and the second is providing an offer to fill that gap. Anything else other than these two is nothing but a waste of time. Whenever I have a phone conversation with a potential client, I would try to listen and understand the gap. I will ask the questions knowing that this is the gap they are working to fill.

During my early days, I tried to fill that gap for them by providing them the solutions on the call, thinking that I am adding value to their life and by doing that they will become my clients. But this was the biggest mistake. You must remember, when you are speaking to a potential client on a diagnosis call, you must never coach them or provide them with a solution. The only job you have on the call is to make a diagnosis like a doctor. Find the gap and provide your offer. If you try to coach them or provide any sort of solution to solve a problem over the phone, they will never buy your services.

You cannot simply solve their problems or fill that gap with the 30-minute phone call. We sometimes believe that if we do not add value or provide a solution, we may lose the client. We believe that by giving value to the clients, they will keep coming back. However, what we don't understand is that they do not return like this. You want to make sure that you do not solve their problems, but rather what you need to do is find the gap for them. The best salespeople do not sell products and services. In fact, the best salespeople sell their desired future to the clients.

THE FAST GROWTH METHOD

The number one rule to growing your business is to make more offers. Most people simply make one or two offers in a month. Due to that, businesses don't grow at the rate they are expected to grow. Don't get attached to your products and services. Many people love talking about their products and their services. Why? Because they have spent so much time and effort in producing them. People think that the more they talk about their product, the more they are able to make a sale. Whenever I spoke to my clients, I used to solve their problems on the strategy call. I used to believe it was my duty to give them some solution even in the first conversation. That is the wrong approach. The only thing you need to do on those diagnosis calls is making sure that you understand the gap and tell them your offer, which can help solve their problem. Some basic rules for making your diagnosis calls are: you must be in a quiet place. You need to be very professional and have those phone calls where you are not interrupted. During my experience with a lot of salespeople, I have noticed that they do not treat their clients professionally. They would conduct diagnosis calls in noisy places like shopping centers or while driving.

You need to be professional when conducting a diagnosis call. One best weapon to make your sales reach the sky is to use silence. People think that by talking more during a sale call, they will get the sale. What works best is to ask a question and be silent. Do not fill the gap by speaking a lot. The silence will be awkward in the beginning. However, that is the requirement in order to make sales.

You are not on the diagnosis call to solve their problems. You are not making the call to coach them. The only thing you need to do is use one word in the entire phone call when your client tells you a problem; *"OK!"*

Clients have so many desired futures. They are confused and have no clarity. They are simply looking for somebody to guide them down a clear path. They do not have the confidence to do it themselves. It is important to set an agenda before the meeting. Most people simply turn up in meetings without a proper agenda in hand. This is a total waste of time.

What Kills the Salespeople?

The first thing is Doubt. Doubt is the number one killer. When a salesperson goes to the market and speaks to five people, and if all five people respond with a NO, the salesperson starts doubting. He doubts that his offer is not right, or the client is not right, or things are not going well. This is what kills the confidence of the salesperson.

Your biggest asset in the sales world is your mindset. If you do not believe that you can sell products worth $2 million, then you will never sell it. It all depends on the mindset. If you do not believe that you can be a good salesperson, then you are right! You will never be able to make sales if you do not believe in yourself.

Another mistake that salespeople do is not gather proper data. Without the required information, you will never be able to make a sale. If you are speaking to somebody, you need to make sure that you are gathering the data of that potential client. When you gather the data, you can re-approach the client later on. I recommend using Hubspot free CRM tool to manage your clients.

Note: "Diagnosis call" – is a phone call with your potential client to convert them into paying client. Do not use the name "Diagnosis call" when booking this meeting with your potential client. This is only for you to understand the reason behind this call. You can name this call whatever you like (except Diagnosis call). Most of our clients just call this "Strategy Call"

Chapter 16
Client Acquisition

"Get closer than ever to your customers. So close, in fact, that you tell them what they need well before they realize it themselves"

- ***Steve Jobs***

In this chapter, we are going to talk about two important things. The first thing is how to get clients or acquire customers organically. The other thing that I am going to discuss in-depth is the tools. In a business, we have different tools for different things and you must be aware of these tools and how they can help you scale your business.

Client Acquisition Methods

We acquire our first few clients through organic ways. In this chapter, I am going to focus on organic ways and how we actually do it. You need to have at least 20% of clients coming organically. So how do you get clients organically?

During the early days, you must start with organic methods. I would never suggest that you should go and start paying for

THE FAST GROWTH METHOD

Facebook Ads or Google Ads. Do not boost or pay for ads. This process is more like a gamble. As you begin to see people liking your posts and people responding to them. You get addicted to that dopamine hit. Therefore, refrain from paying for Facebook Ads until you have least 5-10 paying clients. That dopamine hit will cost you a lot of money. Thus, in order to test your offer and the outcomes, you must start with the organic method. Like I explained, you have a niche market, you know what results they are looking for, and you are filling the gap with your offer. Almost everyone has a Facebook account and has at least 200 people on their friends' list. I am assuming that out of the 200 people, at least 10 of them are in your niche market. You can easily talk to those people and connect with them. This is a small step in gaining clients organically. Do not start with paid ads unless you start acquiring clients in an organic way and tested your offer.

Once you have 5-10 clients and you would like to take it to the next level, then you can start with paid ads. I always tell people that marketing or any money you spend on marketing is not an expense. Marketing should never be an expense. Marketing should always be an investment. If I am spending $1000, I should get something in return, which is more than $1000. Marketing is actually a booster. The more money you invest, the more money you get in return. That's how it should be; however, you need to test it. Your best friend in the entire journey is called *experimentation*. You need to make sure you experiment with everything.

Disadvantages of Organic Methods

Organic reach is very slow. It takes a bit of time because you are going to rely on other people. Organic reach is pretty random. Personally, I do not like the fact that it is so random. The other thing is that it is only good when you are a beginner, and it doesn't create a predictable business. Therefore, make sure that you do not pay for Facebook ads or anything else when you are initially starting. It is advised to start everything slowly and try reaching your community organically.

What are organic methods? Where do we start?

- Start with Facebook posts. Post them on your personal Facebook accounts.
- Upload success stories if you have any.
- Conduct Q&A's
- Find people and add them as friends first.
- Educate your clients.
- Do not always post about business. Keep a 60-40 ratio in mind, where 60% of your posts are about business, and 40% is about other things.

THE FAST GROWTH METHOD

- The most important thing to keep in mind is to do the above-mentioned practices on a daily basis. Be sure to do it consistently.

Facebook post example:

> My $15,000 Giveaway
>
> As you may or may not know, over the last 5 years I have been Coaching people on (your topic). I have also gained (your qualifications). I have decided to give away $15,000 worth of coaching & mentoring to 3 lucky people in my friends list.
>
> I've invested over $50,000 into my own personal development in the last 4 years. But I've since realized that life's too short to not go ALL IN on your dreams and I have since decided to RE-LAUNCH my coaching business.
>
> So, what I'm doing is I'll be looking for 3 people to invest 90 days of my own time and $5,000 each of my own money to help them get the results in
>
> _____
>
> YOU MUST BE WILLING TO INVEST IN YOURSELF TO MAKE THIS WORTHWHILE FOR YOU.
>
> To apply for these 3 spots, comment 'Me' below and I'll get back to you with more details. If you are shy just shoot me a personal message and we will be in touch.
>
> Looking forward to working with you...

You can use the above Post as a template and acquire few clients to test your offer. Once you have delivered your offer and results to your clients, then you can ask for testimonials. The only reason you are giving away your services for free is because you would like to test your offer (services) and collect love (testimonials). If you are already experienced in your field and have already tested your offer and have few testimonials then you can ignore this step.

Another way through which you can get an organic reach is called DMs (Direct Messages). Direct messages work really well with any niche market. However, you should not try to sell them something in the first go, and also, you shouldn't be extra nice to people either and start asking personal questions. Contact people, add them as your friends, and expand your market through DMs. Two basic rules of any DM are:

- Don't be extra nice
- Don't ask them to buy anything

So, what are you supposed to do when you send someone a personalized DM? Invite them. For example, Hey *first name*, I am running this FREE workshop in the city, it is focused on _____, if you find this content useful & relevant, I would love to see you at my event. Or Hey *first name,* I have written this article on *topic* and would love to get your feedback.

E-mail is another option that can be used to connect with people. It is an important tool, and I use it all the time myself. I particularly use a tool called *"Mailchimp."*

Paid Ads

Paid ads give you a very predictable business. As I mentioned earlier, paid marketing should never be considered as an expense. It's an investment for all of us that whenever we put in more money, we expect to get more returns. In our business, the fast growth system works perfectly. At the time of writing this book, every $1 we invest in marketing, giving us a $6 return. It's a system that works now! It means that more paid ads have more returns.

Also, paid ads will give you more consistency. If you look at most of the people in the online world, the same principle is applied. If you invest more, you get returns more. It is a consistent flow. Lastly, it is very easy to scale. I mean it doesn't matter where you live in, you can expand to another level, one after the other. Start with a small database or with a small number of people and then expand further.

One important point to remember is to clean up your Facebook account. In other words, if you have a personal account on Facebook, you need to ensure that all your professional achievements are displayed and visible, and no other activity which deems you as unprofessional ought to be shown. You can add friends and place them in separate lists so that whenever you post about something that you do not want others to see, you can simply hide it. Make your account looks professional.

Business Domain Name

If you are in the business world and running a business, you should have a business domain. By business domain, I mean your own domain name. Your own URL. Also, you shouldn't have a random Gmail address. Being a professional, it is advised to have your own domain name email address since that would show you as a professional to others. Owning a domain doesn't cost much. Let me give you a lesson which I learned the hard way. When you buy a domain name from companies like GoDaddy or any other place, they tell you that you can buy any email from them as well. People who are not aware end up buying an e-mail address from them. If you buy an email service from companies that provide domain, then you should know that their email and SMTP IP address is usually blacklisted by major mail service providers like Gmail, Hotmail, etc. if you send emails from Godaddy SMTP server domains, it is most likely to land in your client's junk mailbox. That is not what you want. You want your clients to get your email in their inbox. So, I suggest that you should have your e-mail hosted on Gmail.com (or GSuite). Website: https://gsuite.google.com

Corporate Clients

I have dealt with the corporate world a lot, and most of the high-level corporate bosses are always behind gatekeepers. So, I couldn't get to those clients during my early days. It's just because there are many gatekeepers before you can get to the right person. What you really need to understand is that, if you are trying to get past the gatekeepers, you need to have a formula or a strategy. A formula that works really well is called bulk post.

If you are dealing with somebody in the corporate space, and you want to reach them and speak directly to a person with authority, Bulk Post (or registered post) works the best. Write down the name by hand and mention your first name only on the sender's address. In the bulk post, send them a letter that states your pitch. This tricks the gatekeeper into thinking that the bulk post is from someone familiar. Therefore, they do not open it and simply forward it to the concerned party.

This trick also works great if you have corporate clients or high-profile clients. If you want to reach people who are not openly available, then this works great. In today's world, people don't send letters or express posts (registered post) anymore. The only things you get in the mailbox these days are bills, so it is a great surprise for people to see something new in the mail. We have tried the same approach to invite high profile clients to our workshops. Also, put our offers in front of many CEO / COO of some major corporations in Australia.

Toolkit

Every business owner must have a toolkit. It is a toolkit of certain tools which makes your life easier. Below are the tools present in the toolkit that I use to enhance my business:

- Facebook: Paid advertisements, my personal account, and my business page, all are essential to run my business.
- Email: Our emails are hosted on Gmail.com or Gsuite.com.
- LinkedIn: This is also another important tool for me in my business.
- MailChimp: It is an e-mail database where you can save all the email addresses of other people. Not a lot of people go through their emails; however, you shouldn't ignore them.
- Instagram: All international businesses that got boosted in the last two years is because of Instagram. I, myself, use Instagram a lot and send DMs to a lot of people.

- Facebook Messenger: There was a time when we read all the emails we received. However, today, we read all the messages we get on FB Messenger. They are of high priority, and that is why almost everyone reads them immediately. Therefore, it is one of the best things that you could use to promote your business. Highly Recommended. You can use Manychat tool for this service
- Clickfunnels: This is our sales funnel tool. I have a website that is designed on WordPress. However, for webinars, events, this book sale, and everything else, I use funnels. Funnels have a better way of directing people from one point to another. As I said, we need people to go through a journey. People will not just understand what you do; you need to take them through it step by step.
- Fiverr: We use Fiverr for any graphic design needs. Before you want people to work for you, you want to get photos nicely edited, banners in place, and other things ready. I got my graphic designing work designed from freelancers at Fiverr. You may have to try few before you get the right candidate for the job.
- Zoom: If you are planning on operating a location free business, and you are looking to speak to people, Zoom is the tool for you. I suggest using 1-on-1 Zoom as it is free of

cost. If you are looking to go LIVE on Facebook or YouTube, Zoom Webinar is a great Add-on.

- WordPress: It is used for static websites. When people tell you that they want to design a website, they usually design them on WordPress. However, I recommend that you do not spend money on Wix and other similar websites. These websites are subscription-based, and you will have to pay on a monthly basis. WordPress is a free service that can be used forever. All you have to do is make a website once and just update its content.
- Textmagic: This tool is helpful in sending bulk texts to people.
- Slack: This is one of my favorite tools. I have to coordinate with my team, which is based globally. Slack helps me coordinate with them, manage them, send them files, and organize everything. You will need this tool especially if you are more than a team of one.
- Zapier – Amazing integration tool
- Hubspot CRM – Every business should have a CRM and Hubspot is certainly the best one and It's FREE!

Joint Ventures (JVs)

When you are earning a good amount of revenue, and you are

considering taking it to the next level, I would recommend having a joint venture strategy. Who do think you can JV with?

It is a great idea to start speaking to those who serve the similar target market as you do but provide different type of solutions. For example: Accountants are perfect partnership clients for us because they serve the similar clients as we do but provide very different type of service compare to us.

Moving on, I want you to make a list of the tools that you have in your toolkit. You have to identify the tools that are going to help you succeed. Write down the first three tools that come to your mind. Once you reach that phase where your business is booming, it will be easier for you to know what step to take as those tools will help you in making the appropriate decisions.

However, if you do not know what you want and if you haven't identified the right set of tools, then it is going to be hard to achieve what you seek. You can always refer to the list that I have mentioned earlier about the tools I use. You can then select the top three tools that you think will be the best fit for you.

At the end, I would like to remind you that you must remember the experts trap. Tools are good to have but they won't bring clients to your business. Your first priority should be getting few clients, testing your offer and collecting love.

▶ Most frequently asked questions ….

Question: Shall I build website or lead magnet first?

Answer: Always build Lead Magnet first! Use Clickfunnels

Don't spend time building a big website first. Give them what they want as a lead magnet.

Question: What the average price to build a website?

Answer: WordPress / Clickfunnels - $2000USD or less.

Question: Where to hire experts to do logo, website, any other minor technical jobs?

Answer: Fiverr.com is the best place.

Chapter 17
Proof of Concept (PoC)

"Don't find customers for your products, find products for your customers"

- Seth Godin

People who come from a corporate background are very aware of the word PoC. Let's say you have a niche market. To get results for the niche market, you have a number of offers before you have one offer that works best. You have to go through many different offers before you could find the perfect one. Proof of Concept is a simple term where we create a proof of concept with a number of people in your list, email contacts, niche market, and you try using that offer with them (test market). You get their feedback and improve your product before you release it to the external world.

Now and then I get to meet interesting people. Some of them attend my workshops, and some I meet online. When you talk to them, they are looking for a partnership. They have a million-dollar idea, and they are looking for a partner who can coach them and mentor them and do their marketing.

The first thing I always ask people who are looking for a partnership is, did you go through the process and served at least 20 clients? Usually, the answer is No. They want to JV with someone to scale their business, but they haven't tried their offer with anyone yet. The result is nothing but a waste of time. You must try your formula / product / offer with at least 5-10 people organically and make changes before you release it to the wider audience.

Client Acquisition Methods

I explained this strategy in the earlier chapters too; however, I will go through this again. I have a strategy that I use for my company and for our clients. So, when you invest in a paid ad, the paid ad has to go somewhere and show some value. What we do is that we show some sort of value by doing a series of videos. You can opt for PDF downloads, a webinar, a master class or anything that has high value for your clients. The reason for doing so is for the Facebook ad to give people some great value. Once the value has been delivered, you can take them further.

You can invite them for a phone call, join a Facebook group, or invite them for an online event. You can do it in any way you like, and the only condition is that you do something. This is how it works. You have a Facebook ad, you give some sort of value, and then you ask for something at the end. I always say the ratio of give

& take must be 80-20. 80% Give value, and 20% ask for business in return.

To understand this in-depth, you need to understand a concept. This concept must be understood before you go into Paid Ads. Pressing the "Boost" button may not cost much in the beginning, but in no time, it will start taking money from your bank account without you even knowing it. So, don't press the "Boost" button! Marketing is a vast term to understand. If you have been marketing for a while, there are three types of people out there, depending on the type of industry that you are a part of. 10% of the people just won't buy from you. No matter how much you try, they just won't buy from you at all, or they might just buy from your competition. There is 80% of the population that is in the middle and is not ready to buy right now.

And then there is the other 10% of the population that is ready to buy right now or will be ready in next 30 days. They have a problem, and they are aware that they have a problem, due to which they are looking for a solution. They are ready to buy right now. Most business owners market to the 10% who are ready to buy right now, but they ignore the big 80% chunk that will be ready to buy very soon. Let's look at it how we can market to those...

There are two types of marketing methods:

- Perception Marketing (Brand building)
- Direct Marketing

Perception marketing refers to targeting 80% of the market mentioned earlier. These people are the ones who are not ready to buy today, but they will be ready soon. So what we do is we build this perception in the marketplace that when they face a problem, they think of you. This is what we call perception marketing.

Perception marketing is creating a certain perception about you and your brand in the marketplace, so that people get to know you, like you, trust you, and want what you are selling.

Direct marketing is nothing more than telling people what to do and directing them toward something. We tell them what to do, whether it is clicking on the link or booking a call, booking a ticket for your upcoming event. That is direct marketing. Direct marketing is always targeted toward 10% of the people who are ready to buy right now.

Let's look at Google. Most businesses use Google to do direct marketing; however, on Facebook you can do both direct and perception marketing together. You can build your brand and do direct marketing, as well.

Google Ads vs Facebook Ads

THE FAST GROWTH METHOD

In Google Ads, most people search by category instead of searching by name. For example, they will type 'Plumber' in the google search instead of a very specific plumber name.

I truly believe that when somebody searches me on Google, they shouldn't search me under a category. Instead, they should find me by my name. For example, somebody searches for *"Business Coach"* in the area, and my name pops up. Personally, I am not aiming for that at all. What I want from Google is that people should search for me by my name. They should type "Jag Jassel" in the search bar, and they should see me and posts related to me. Google used to be important, and I believe that it still is for certain businesses, but today, Facebook is a much better tool, saying that, next few years, there will be another tool that might replace Facebook.

Why Facebook is a better tool today? There are two reasons behind it. You can do perception marketing and direct marketing both on Facebook. You can do both at the same time. This is very important because if you are a business owner, you just don't want to sell like crazy. You also want to build your reputation and brand.

The other reason is that Facebook can track everything. It can track people's behavior and advertise according to that behavior. You can target if someone believes in a certain way or if someone is interested in a certain thing.

Whatever I am mentioning in this chapter are not just theories. We are applying these on a daily basis for hundreds of our clients and for our business.

Before you think of starting your Facebook Ads, there are certain things that are required:

- Setup your Business Name
- Create a Facebook Business Page
- Your own Business Domain Name
- Setup your Email for your Business Domain. Make sure that your email is associated with your domain; however it is under G-suite or Gmail as they are the best ones in my opinion.
- Funnels. These are helpful in guiding the visitors to your website.
- Also, you need a proper payment integration. If you want to accept payment online. I recommend Stripe
- Set up your email automation system. When people register on your website, where does that email go? As I mentioned earlier, you can use MailChimp, which is completely free to use.
- Facebook Bot – Not mandatory, but highly recommended. Use the Manychat tool for any Facebook Messenger automation.

What Mistakes I was Making?

Many years ago, when I started my journey, I had this thought that I have to do a lot of things before I can get clients for my business. I was doing podcasts, blogs, Facebook Live, social media posts, etc. I was spending so much of my time writing blogs and creating new content. Most of my time in the day was spent doing very random things.

However, along the way, I learned to focus on one thing only. This is something that I heard from a friend of mine. Generally, a lot of people spend most of their time on social media. They want to do many things. But they never ask themselves, *"Do I want to be a millionaire, or do I want to just look like a millionaire?"*

A lot of people seem to be millionaires. Their lifestyle shows that they might be millionaires. Now let me ask you, do you want to be a millionaire or you just want to look like one? Because most just pretend to be a millionaire. You want to make sure that you don't get consumed in all the other shiny stuff. You don't want to pretend to be one; you actually want to be a successful millionaire. The moment I understood this concept, I came to the realization that I was putting so much time into looking like a millionaire instead of working on what actually makes money. Today, all I do is work on my craft. My craft is my first priority, and everything else is nothing but a waste of time. For me, my craft is educating others. I teach and train people, and I love doing that.

This is what makes me, Me! I do that every day. I spend all my time preparing, planning, and designing content for my trainings and workshops, and then I deliver it. I forget everything else and simply focus on what I love and what gets my money rolling. Why? Because that is my priority, and I spend most of my time on it. I truly believe in the law of 10,000 hrs. It means that 10,000 hours of "deliberate practice" are needed to become world-class in any field. The same applies to you too. What is your craft?

Sportspeople are the biggest example for us. If you go and take a look at any world-class sports player who is known for their sports, all they do is practice their craft. They may have a very average looking website, and a Facebook page which is not updated, why? The answer is because they don't spend time doing things that are useless to them. They are mostly working out in gyms or swimming in pools or having practice matches. They are doing what they are supposed to be doing, working on their craft. Therefore, do not waste your time on these tools. Yes, they are important, and you need to do that too. However, this is not going to make you successful. They are nothing but tools. These tools will take your business to the next level, but you don't have to waste all of your time on them. Pay attention to your craft and work on it on a daily basis.

Work on what helps your roll in money. Remember that everything else is nothing but a waste of time. Therefore, work on your superpower as that is what will bring you success and money. I remember my mentor telling me this: *"As a business owner, we have only two things to do. Everything else is a waste of time. The two things are: find new customers, and find a way to retain your existing customers."*

Most people spend a lot of time understanding tools, implementing them, making banners, working on their websites and other stuff rather than working on the most important part of the business, i.e. getting clients and helping them get the results. A doctor is a perfect example of this. A doctor may have hundreds of tools with him. However, those tools are useless if the doctor has no knowledge about how to treat a patient. Therefore, tools are only useful if you know how to properly utilize them to help your clients get results.

In order to get a client, you need to know about their journey. You need to find out exactly where they sit, where they hang out before they come to you.

Let's talk about organic reach. If you are looking for clients and you don't have any clients, my question is where is your clientele?

Where are your clients gathered today? Where do they go and meet before they come to you?

Chapter 18
Taking Your Business to the Next Level

"Customer experience better be at the top of your list when it comes to priorities in your organization. Customer experience is the new marketing."

– *Steve Cannon*

In this chapter, I will cover a little about the technical things, along with discussing what I would do in certain situations if I have to start everything from zero again.

That being said, we will discuss the following:

- Funnels – Sales funnels
- Offer – How to create a No Brainer Offer. This means that people should not have to think about buying your product after you have given your offer.
- My 9-Step formula that will take your business from zero to the next level. For that, you will have to strictly follow my formula. If you miss any one of them, it will not work. If someone gives you a recipe, most of the time, people add in

their own experiences. This is what ruins the recipe. Therefore, do not bring your experience into this. Just follow it step by step. Once you have experience in this system, then you can add / update any of the steps. But in the beginning, just following the system!

Sales Funnels

Funnel is one of the best decisions that you could make for your business. I am going to talk about sales funnels and the process that comes with it. Why is the Sales funnel so important? The reason is that our entire goal is on its journey. Whenever you acquire a client, you have to take your clients on a journey. You cannot simply expect them to buy something from you without going on a journey. Funnels are a perfect tool for that purpose.

You need to understand funnels and design the steps and the journey. Funnels are what will help you fill that gap and automate the process; however, you need to know the steps to it. You are the person who is taking the customer on a journey; funnels don't. The funnel is only a tool that aids in that journey. So, you need to design the steps first. Most people have this perception that funnels will do everything for them. However, the sale funnel is just the tool, and you need to create the journey before that.

Website vs. Funnel

I get asked this question most of the time. What is the difference between a website and a funnel? A website is very static. It is like a notice board where people can simply come and read about you or your business. A funnel acts as your personal assistant who walks you through the university, school, or shopping mall. You can read on the notice board or website to find out about where you should go. Like you go back and touch the screen that has a map of the mall. The map will help you locate yourself and give you directions to where you want to go. However, a funnel acts like a person who will hold your hand and take you through your journey instead of you having to go through it alone. That is why I think that funnels are very important.

Remember, people do not have a very long attention span. They will go through your website, stay there for thirty seconds or less, and then move on to the next. You need to guide them through the process. When you do that, they are more likely to buy from you rather than your competitors. There was a time when there used to be a much bigger search engine before Google. That search engine company was Yahoo! It was the biggest company in the world at that time. They had a search engine; however, when you go to Yahoo's front page to search something, you would find more than 200+ other links on their front page.

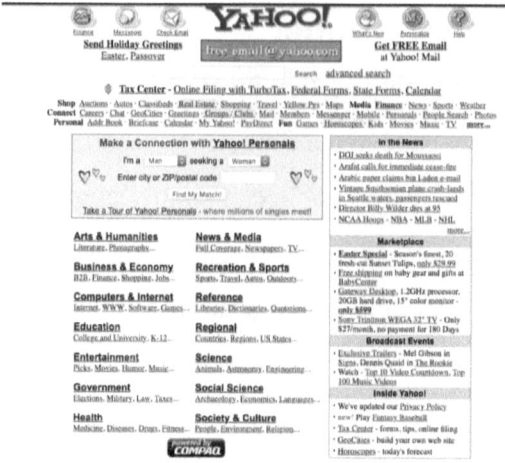

(2002 yahoo front page example)

Google, on the other hand, then came and put only one search tab link in front of you, the search bar. Nothing else. That is the difference between a website and a funnel. I recommend everyone to have a funnel if they are looking to establish their business and take it to the next level.

The Secret Formula

This is a secret formula to create a funnel. I got this formula from Russell Brunson. The secret formula is all about who your target market is, where they stand before they come to you, what your offer is, and what are the results they are seeking.

Before creating a funnel, there are some questions that need to be answered. Questions include:

- **Who is your dream client? Who do you want to serve?**

You do not create a product first and decide who to sell it to later. You focus on your target market, and then you create a product for them. Most people make this mistake, which is why they find it really hard to sell their product or service. The reason is they start from the wrong side of the equation.

- **Where are they gathering? Where do they hang out?**

If you are a person who is associated with coaches, the health industry, or the IT industry, you need to find where they hang out on the internet or in person. If you are associated with the technology industry, the people there would be hanging out on different technology websites, technology events, or on technology forums.

- **What can I create?**

What can I offer them so they can pick my bait?

- **What results do they want to get?**

Business owners believe that their products and services are the number one thing, and they matter the most to their clients. In reality your products and services have no meaning at all. Clients care more about the outcome. They care about what results they will get after they use your product or service. They are least concerned about what name you have given to your product or what product you have.

What I am trying to explain is: you should not spend so much time worrying about the name or the packaging or the color of the product. You should work on the results as that is what the clients are really concerned about. As I have mentioned earlier in the book that the business that is able to take the customers to their desired outcome quicker and faster makes more money. What mistakes do most people make? More & more people spend way too much time learning some sh*t that will not serve their clients in anyway.

Once they have learned it, they go ahead and create a product using the information they have learned. Then, the end outcome is always nothing but sh*t everywhere. That is why businesses do not work. As I said, most businesses are started by employees. The employee's mind only thinks about their skillset and how they can use their skillset to earn money. Therefore, you should not spend so much time creating a product and think that people will just buy your product. Let me give you an example of my business journey. I was really good at technology, so my first preference has always been building technology platforms to start any business. I spent months and months creating those platforms, hiring external developers to develop those programs but no time on sales & marketing.

Hence, the business had no chance. I didn't make this mistake once or twice but 13 times. (What can I say, I am a slow learner) I will repeat myself again and again until you have understood this concept clearly. So, there is a niche market, and the niche market has a desired future. They are looking to get to the desired future *FAST*, and there is a GAP, which we call it **The Gap**. You are the person who fills the gap with your offer. Your offer is what will take them from point A to point B. Therefore, the most important thing in this space is your client's desired future. You need to remember that your niche market does not matter much and your offer doesn't matter either. What matters the most is the desired results of your niche market. That is what they are expecting you to deliver to them.

If you are running a business that is providing service, you must always keep the desired results in mind. If you do not understand this concept and spend all your time working on the offer, then you are going to miss out. You need to forget yourself and take yourself out of the picture. Find out where your potential client wants to go, so you can take them there.

Let's take a look at the internet. You may remember that I asked earlier where your target audience gathers before they come to you. They gather at a number of different places. Once you know that the next step is to bring them at your place and take them through the journey starting from Step 1, Step 2, and Step 3 and so on. There will be people who will drop out of that process. It doesn't mean that you have to serve everybody. It simply means that some people are going to leave your journey. Sales is an elimination process. So you put a process together to qualify prospects. Those who are going to be right at the end are the perfect clients; they are the ones ready to take on your offer.

I didn't understand this concept earlier in my journey and helped people to get to a desired future. When they bought my product, after sometime they came back to me for more, but I didn't have a product to sell to them. Then I realized that you take your clients on a journey because they are looking for somebody like you. You need to understand that there is no one destination, but rather you take them on a journey.

Your Offer

As a business owner, you should never talk about your offer first. For your offer to act as a vehicle, you must know the destination your prospects are looking to get to and carefully place your offer as a vehicle. When you make an offer, it means that you are hitting it on the mark telling them that they have a problem, and you have the solution to it. The buyer should think that if they want their problem to be solved, then they have to simply buy your product or service. But how do we create that offer? In order to create an offer, there are three things in the marketplace to keep in mind.

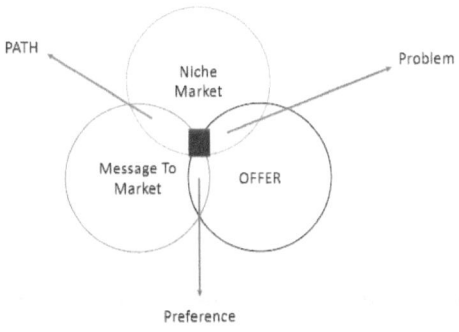

You have a niche market, you have an offer, and you have a message. In the figure above, there are some intersecting points where some of the circles overlap. Wherever the circle is overlapping between the niche market and your offer, then that depicts the problem they are facing. Your niche market has many problems; however, it does not mean that you give them offers that will help solve all the problems out there. You only pick one problem and offer a solution to that. Where there is an intersection between the niche market and the offer, you pick one problem in that space. Second, if you take a look at the space overlapping between offer and message to the market, then that space is called the preference. Preference refers to how your clients prefer to get a message communicated to them. How do they want to receive messages? Do they prefer it to be said in a certain way, or do they want it in a specific lingo?

Lastly is the space between the message to the market and the niche market. That space is known as the path. What is their pathway? How are you going to deliver that? What are the steps to take? You can notice that all three circles intersect at one place, which is marked with a red square. That place with the red square is the perfect offer with the perfect message to market for your niche market. That is where you are speaking to the right people with the right solution and with the right message to the market.

How to Create an Offer?

What do you need to include in that offer? What are the ingredients for that offer? How do you make that offer? Your offer must have *a recipe*. It must have your recipe. Anybody can solve a problem. If a client goes to anyone related to the industry, they can get their problem solved. There are many people available to do the work. However, what you are looking for is that your prospects keep coming to you to get that specific problem solved. For that you need to create a certain recipe where people can see how you solve the problem. For example, anyone can bake a cake. But why do people buy Jamie Oliver's books for a cake recipe? No matter the cook book, the cake remains the same. The cake may taste different but you will get a cake in the end. However, everybody has their own recipe. Therefore, the question for you is, what is your recipe? Once you have created a recipe (system), you must give a name to that recipe. In our world, we have a recipe called the fast growth system. This book is designed to provide you the entire recipe.

After that, you need a support system to help them implement your recipe. Everybody and anybody can give you the recipe. A lot of 'How-to' recipes are available on the Internet these days. But what people are looking for is a support system along with the recipe to answer any questions that they might have along the journey. Therefore, the question for you is what support system do you have in place for those who are ready to follow your recipe?

People are always in need of support. People are in search of a good support system. And then another point to consider is what tools do you bring to the table? The reason for having a certain set of tools is to help you take things to the next level. In the end, you are giving the clients the results they are looking for. That is how you make an offer.

So how do you create an offer? You clearly identify what your niche market's current situation is. You need to clearly tell where they are today. What does point A look like? And what is point B? Where does your niche market want to go towards? What is their desired future? What is their point B? By answering these questions, you are aware of point A and point B and you can easily fill that gap. What happens is that most business owners take their clients everywhere except for their desired destination. You should not be one of those people who is just roaming around in circles thinking that they are going somewhere. Going around does not help you or your clients. The only thing you are doing is wasting too much time.

Remember one thing, just like any other human being, everybody has many desires. Everybody wants so many things. Since a lot of people are very confused, therefore they want something but they are not aware of what they want. Your job is to find out what exactly they are looking for by asking them the right questions. Quality questions are what is going to build your business. These questions are referred to be the million-dollar questions. When these million-dollar questions are answered, you will be making a million dollars too.

However, one thing to keep in mind is that you should not offer solutions for all the problems they have. You are offering a solution to only one problem to begin with. In the future, you may expand and offer something else, however you need to ensure to take them through one journey and not many journeys at a time.

Offer includes: Your recipe + Tools + Support System

How to create your Secret Recipe (Secret Sauce)

In order to create your recipe, you need steps. So what are the steps for taking your client from point A to point B? How are you planning on taking them forward? What tools do you think they will need? What support would they need throughout this journey? What belief should they have? What belief should they let go of? What do they need to learn?

After you have are designed your offer, you provide your clients three delivery options:

- You give them the recipe for free and they do the rest themselves. For example: At our Fast Growth Event, we share our recipe with everyone who attends the event for FREE and they can take away the entire recipe and implement themselves.
- You help them implement your recipe step by step with you in a group session – For example: Our **Fast Growth Program**, which is a 90 days program to help business owners get started on this path or our **Champions Club** providing continuous support and helping them take their business to the next level.
- 1-on-1 - Some people may even want to work with you on 1-on-1 to get to their desired future FAST. For Example: My

private consulting where I work personally with clients to help them grow their business *FAST*!

Therefore, you need to design three levels of delivery for the same offer. You may have only one delivery model at the moment, however you need to start thinking about how you can implement these three delivery models in your business.

Here's is the ONE question I get asked the most. If I am at zero today, standing at the starting line, what would I do?

So here are my steps if I am starting from day 1 (at zero)

- Step 1 - Figure out who do I want to serve.
- Step 2 – What is their current situation? In order to answer this question, I will to speak to my target audience directly and determine their problems, frustrations, desires, goals, dreams issues, and motivations. I will go out and conduct my market research. Next, I would go and analyze which five companies are in my industry serving the same clients and solving their problems today. What are their offers, delivery model and price points? And then I will do what most of you must get used to it. Buy your competitors products / services to understand the entire end-to-end process.
- Step 3 – What are their desired future? So after I interview them and get to know them I will determine what their

desired future is and where they want to go. They will tell me many problems but I will pick only one out of them (generally the most common one).

- Step 4 - Create a No Brainer offer. After speaking to my prospects and determining what exactly their problem is, and what motivates them, I then look into my competition. I analyze what my competition is doing, what are they offering and then make something better in comparison to them.
- Step 5 – Create a proven recipe. I will come up with my step by step recipe. In other words, how can I take them step by step from their current situation to the desired future. It would be my step by step process added with mindset along with a support system i.e. (Recipe + Support + Tools). All of these things added together will help create my presentation.
- Step 6 – Presentation. I will now create my *belief building presentation* (chapter 23) and it will contain exactly what I will present to my niche market. I will show them how I will be able to solve their problem, step by step.
- Step 7 – Value Stack. In this step, I will move on to create my value stack, which would be based on my recipe, my offer, and my bonuses. In other words, what else my target audience required to get to their desired future. For example, I know that as a coach if you are starting out you will need

an event or webinar funnel, logo design and client contracts. So I will offer that as bonus at the end of my presentation.

- Step 8 – Event. I will organize a workshop and spend most of my time and money promoting that event. Whether it's online or offline, I will conduct these workshops where I can present my recipe to people.
- Step 9 – Action. Lastly, I will now do the work. I will physically go out and deliver my presentation. I will speak to as many people as possible and show them my recipe. I'm a huge believer of massive action and it is time to take the action.

On a side note, after few presentations when my model start to work, I will automate the entire process and get people to book some time in my calendar.

Here's the summary of my 9-step process:

- Who do I want to serve?
- What is their current situation?
- What is their desired future?
- No brainer offer
- My proven recipe
- Presentation
- Value stack

- Event/Workshop/Masterclass
- Action

If I am going through this process, my next priority will be to get the results. As I will receive feedback, I will make the necessary changes in the offer accordingly. Lastly, I will collect Love. By that I mean, I will collect testimonials.

Then I will go ahead and repeat the entire process:

- Conduct an event/workshop/masterclass
- Take action
- Systemize online
- Automate online
- Hire salespeople to replicate the work I started.

Chapter 19
Focus and the Millionaire Path

"Become a millionaire not for the million dollars, but for what it will make of you to achieve it."

— *Jim Rohn*

In this chapter, I will emphasize only one word, **Focus**. Wherever your focus goes, your energy flows. Your energy is going to flow in the direction where your focus is.

Keep this in mind, in your business, or even in life; you have to focus on certain things. If you do not focus on certain important parts of life, or business, the outcome will not be what you expected. That is how nature is. When you plant a seed, you need a certain focus on very specific things for it to grow. Once it has grown, your focus will change to different things / tasks. In the same way, business, life, and relationships have the same rule.

You must learn to focus on specific tasks in your business at certain levels. The following is the path to create million-dollar businesses. This will explain what you must focus on at different stages of your business.

The Millionaire Path

When people start their journey, they go through a certain path to reach it. I will discuss this path that will help you create a million-dollar business. You need to understand the step-by-step process and what happens in each of the steps.

A lot of people speak about being an entrepreneur or investor. These are the stages that we all target. You cannot simply skip to being an entrepreneur from day 1. You need to walk all the steps. Some people may be on different stages in life. Therefore, you need to identify where you stand in your business path today so you can easily focus on certain things.

Seeker

The first stage is *"Seeker."* Seekers are those people who are not aware of what they actually want. They go from place A to B to C, looking for something. Even though they look for something, they don't really know what they want. That is why they are called seekers because they are seeking something.

A few years ago, even I was a seeker. That is because every business that I started, I was failing in that. I was trying to understand which way to go. I knew where I stood, and I knew that I didn't want to stand in that place. I knew what I didn't want, but I didn't know what I actually wanted.

Seekers are those people who go to different places, attend different events; they check out different things, attend investment workshops, attend cryptocurrency events, or meditation meetups. They are the ones who want to learn about technology, funnels, marketing, website building, etc. They want to do everything because they are not sure of what they want. They have no idea. We all start at being seekers.

As a seeker, what are the things we need to do? What are the questions we need to ask? What do we need to focus on? Once we have identified these things, then you would realize that these are the things we have to focus on. Therefore, we need to understand the things we must do as a seeker.

The first thing seekers need to understand is the questions that they need to ask. If you want to move from seeker to apprentice, the question you need to be asking yourself all the time is, *"Who am I?"* Your focus should always be on your self-identity. What do you stand for? What are your values? What do you like? What do you not like? This is what a seeker does. Also, there is a fallback question. Seekers fall back after facing the question, "How do I stop pressure and noise?"

Most people are just like everybody else because they are dabbling. The time they are spending as a seeker, they are mostly dabbling. They go from one point to another point and tackle different fields, which is fine. However, being a seeker who wants to move to the next level, you need to keep asking yourself the same question, "Who am I?"

SEEKER	
Fallback Question	How do I stop pressure and noise?
Go Forward Question	Who Am I?
Time	Dabbling
Focus	Self-Identity

Apprentice

Moving on, when you are past the seeker stage, and you are on the next level, how do you find that you are an apprentice and not a seeker anymore. You have chosen a path.

When you are an apprentice, most people started asking questions like, *"I could have chosen this path."* You could have done anything, but this is where you are. Most people start getting frustrated and wonder why they are doing this. When you are in such a place, you need to ask yourself, *"How do I become an entrepreneur?"*

Being an apprentice, your focus should be on your skillset and your value creation. When you are an apprentice, you need to completely focus on developing your skillset. If you want to become a life coach, your focus should be on life coaching skills. In that space, most people are apprentices in their part-time. So, once you start your journey as a seeker, then that would indicate you have chosen a path for yourself and are now an apprentice.

APPRENTICE	
Fallback Question	What is wrong with me?
Go Forward Question	How do I become an entrepreneur?
Time	Part Time
Focus	Skill and Value Creation

Promoter

When people become a promoter, they worry about getting ahead. They start asking questions like, "How do I get ahead?" When you become a promoter, you start dealing with Facebook ads;

you start dealing with people outside your business, you start conducting workshops, you start coming out to the world and tell them about you and your business.

In this situation, the question you should be asking yourself is, *"Who is my tribe?"* You figure out who you are going to serve. If you want to move forward, you need to build your tribe. In the 21st century, due to social media, we have no customers and no clients. People buy only from their tribes. People do not buy from random businesses anymore. You have to build a tribe. It doesn't matter if you build it physically or just in your mindset. People connect with those who they believe are a part of their tribe. There are some who only buy from their communities. Others prefer buying from only a certain kind of people.

As a promoter, what should you be focusing on? You should be focusing on Marketing and Sales. Therefore, if you have a business that is up and running, and you are promoting that business, your main focus should be its ***marketing and sales***. Everything else is a waste of time. This is the phase where you transition from part-time to working full-time in your business.

PROMOTER

Fallback Question	How do I get ahead?
Go Forward Question	Who is my tribe?
Time	Full Time
Focus	Marketing and Sales

Self-Employed

The next level is the self-employed level. This is the level where you have a business up and running, and you are making money. However, because of that, you are working too much. You end up working overtime. This is where you should be focusing on automating your sales and marketing. On this level, you should ask yourself the question, "How do I make money?" instead of asking, "How do I move further?"

SELF EMPLOYED	
Fallback Question	How do I get further ahead?
Go Forward Question	How do I make money?
Time	Overtime
Focus	Automated Marketing and

Operator

You become an operator when you have a team member and have delegated your work. A few years ago, I was at the operator level because I had about 16 team members to whom I delegated most of my work. I had the leverage going on. As an operator, you need to be asking, "How do I get leverage?" Your focus, in this space, should be on putting together a business system.

➡ On a side note: Watch my training on my YouTube channel: "5 MUST Have Business System For You To Grow Your Business"

In this phase, you must have a virtual assistant. When you have started to make money, you need to have a virtual assistant. You may ask why, and the answer is because you do not want to be playing the role of an admin. When you become the admin of your own company, you begin losing track of what is important. A virtual assistant is one of the significant expenses you need to make once you start earning money. You need to start delegating your work at this time of your journey. This is how the operator's mind works.

OPERATOR	
Fallback Question	How does my team get me ahead?
Go Forward Question	How do I get leverage?
Time	Delegate time
Focus	Delivery systems

Leader

Now that you have started delegating your work, and you have your team members, the next thing you need to do is to think about, "How do I grow this team?" As a leader, your job is to grow your team. This is where the transformation of leadership comes into place. Now let me talk about the BIG problem. If you have come from the corporate world, you are the most likely to be the victim of this problem. The quick answer to this big problem is a clash of identity. Let me give you an example.

When I used to work for companies like IBM and Oracle, I was a leader. My job was to manage and grow my team. I had different team members, and I helped them in growing, organizing things, whereas they helped me in doing my job appropriately. Once I left that job, I still stayed in that 'leader' identity. I forgot that I needed to take the leadership hat off and have the apprentice hat on.

I didn't know this clash of identity earlier, and a lot of people out there who are starting their business are not aware of it either. This is what hurts the most because you were a leader where you had a team, and now all of a sudden, you are alone and have to start from the beginning again. So you must remember, if you left your corporate job to start a new business, you must also shift your identity from being a leader to a seeker or apprentice otherwise you will always stay in pain.

LEADER	
Fallback Question	How does my team get ahead?
Go Forward Question	How do I grow my team?
Time	Delegate success
Focus	Transformational leadership

Owner

The real definition of a business owner is that he can go away for a month or two, and the business still runs smoothly. That is why it is called the "Autonomy of Time." The business owner does not have to worry about the business when he/she is away. Most people say that they are business owners, but the truth is, they are still employees in their business. The business owners I am referring to are the ones who leave their workplace and do not come back for months, yet the business is still running. They focus on culture, recruiting, and team development.

Business owners are not worried about the timespan. They work as they please. Also, most of the business owners ask themselves this question when moving forward, *"How do I grow my business?"*

OWNER	
Fallback Question	How does my team get further ahead?
Go Forward Question	How do I grow my business?
Time	Give up autonomy of time
Focus	Culture, Recruiting and Team Development

Investor

The investor is one who has the money and free time. They look for places where they can invest and reap most benefits from. When I became successful for the first time, I moved on to become an investor. I had free time in my hands, and I had the money to invest. Therefore, I invested. I started to replicate my success in order to be more successful.

So how do I replicate my success? I started with something else. I had the money and the time, so I thought, *how can I maximize my return on time?* As an investor, the focus is on the Scale.

INVESTOR	
Fallback Question	How do we help others get ahead?
Go Forward Question	How do I replicate my success?
Time	Maximize Return on Time
Focus	Scale

Entrepreneur

The entrepreneur stage is the last stage, where you need to accomplish many things. How do you know that you have reached the entrepreneur stage? There is no time limit when you are an entrepreneur. Your focus is mostly on building your legacy and contributions. For example, Bill Gates. If you notice, he only talks about his contributions and his legacy. The only thing he does is think of ways to contribute even more. The question that entrepreneurs ask themselves is, *"How do I make the greatest contribution?"*

ENTREPRENEUR	
Fallback Question	How do we help everyone?
Go Forward Question	How do I make my greatest contribution?
Time	Giveaway Leveraged Time
Focus	Maximize Legacy and Contribution

The above-mentioned are the different stages of becoming an entrepreneur. I suggest that you learn these stages and utilize them as much as you can in your journey to your business' success. For example, if you are a promoter, you need to focus on your marketing and sales. And if you are an apprentice, you need to focus on your skillset. Regardless of which stage you are in, you should focus on that specific aspect.

Chapter 20
Bridging the Gap

"Quantum mind practice is a transcendent practice into the future self, and it is all about building a new character particle by particle"

– Jag Jassel

In this chapter, I will be sharing a tool that I have been using for the past seven years. That tool is one of the best things I have discovered, and I believe that if you use that tool, it will open up an abundance in whatever you are looking for in your life. It can be a business success, a relationship, an abundance of money, or anything that you may be looking for. I truly believe that this tool has that power because I have witnessed people using it and even I have used it for the past many years in a very specific way and have received visible results.

This chapter is all about Bridging the Gap. I have discussed a lot about this in the previous chapters that everyone has a current view of the world and the desired future. Each and every one of us wants to become something in a certain way. In between, there is a gap that comes in. So how do we fulfill that gap quicker and faster for ourselves? Yes, we all want to do it for our clients, but before we learn to do it for our clients, we need to learn to do it for ourselves.

How do I fill that gap? Where do I create that bridge, so the gap does not remain a gap? A bridge is what connects two different banks of a river. Similarly, I am going to explain about that bridge that connects the current situation to the desired future. Remember that everybody lives in the gap; however, people are not aware of it. And that is where the trouble comes in when people don't know that they are living in the gap. So how do we fix the gap?

Human Beings Live in the Gap for Their Entire Life

As mentioned earlier, everyone lives in the gap, which is why most of the people are not happy nowadays. The worst part is that people don't know that they are living in the gap. The reason is that they believe they will be happy once they acquire something specific.

However, what they are not aware of is that the moment they achieve their desire, another desire arises. This is a continuous process that goes on and on. People have this "If-then" condition in their life, meaning if this happens, then they will be happy. What they don't know is that another desired future arises as soon as one has been fulfilled. Without this desired future, humans won't be able to survive. Thereby, one can say that having a desired future is essential for human existence.

Some might say that humans should not have desires. However, I say that human beings are born in a way that they go toward the desired future. Even if you are sitting in a jungle, you still have a desired future. There is always something that you want or somewhere that you want to get to. Without this desired future, human beings are not able to survive.

What Did the Monks, Sages and Gurus Discover?

If you read old books and scriptures, they claim that we live in a time of "duhkha," which means that we live in this "affliction" world of suffering. To understand "duhkha," we need to understand "sukha," which means "pleasure." So what is this world of pleasure today?

In Sanskrit, "sukha" translates to "happiness," "ease," or "bliss." It is just like one side of the coin, and "duhkha" is the other side of it. No matter how thin the coin is, you will always have both sides. So why is there so much suffering in the world? Wherever there is happiness, there will also be unhappiness and suffering.

Values & Beliefs

Time and time again, it has been mentioned repeatedly in several chapters regarding the different views of the world. We all have our own view of the world that has been built and enhanced by different factors such as family, friends, and society.

Even though you are from the same country as your family and friends. However, you have been given a different set of values and beliefs. With time, you will die defending those values and beliefs. Any war ongoing today has nothing to do with any God or religion.

These fights are because people want to prove their point and enforce their view of the world on other people. They believe in a certain way, and they want other people to believe the same too. That is where the problems arise because people defend their values and beliefs until they die. It is said that if you give a child a religion till the age of 7, he will defend that religion for the rest of his life. This is the biggest issue. All of us have started living in that mindset. Due to this different view of the world, we have all developed a thing called "expectations." I truly believe that these "expectations" are the cause of all suffering in the world.

This happens because when you have a certain view of the world, you want others to believe, behave, and act the same way as you do. When others do not do things according to your values and beliefs, you suffer. And when people do as you believe, you are happy, and you gain pleasure.

This means that we live our entire lives imposing our values and beliefs on other people and want them to act in a certain way. It is being done almost everywhere. Wherever there is an expectation, there is misery.

Live your life as an observer and not as a participant in any action. Live it as a third person. When you do that, the biggest advantage is that nothing hits you personally. I can strongly say that people who live their lives as an observer, they are the happiest.

The Path to Quantum Mind

I have talked about it a lot that there is a monkey mind and a quantum mind. We have a journey to cover, and there is a gap in between. We all want to fill that gap between the monkey mind and the quantum mind. There are tools that may help in filling that gap. In this chapter, I am going to discuss how you can reach that point as an individual with a quantum mind.

Firstly, I want you to understand the whole concept on an intellectual level since it is an intellectual book. Intellectually, you can transcend to that state where you have a quantum mind, and the only way of achieving that is through "meditation."

Meditation is a word that is overly used in today's society. Nowadays, there are two types of people; those who meditate and those who don't. There is no in-between. Some people love meditating, whereas some people may have tried it and did not like it.

Meditation is not just one way or thing. It is a vast world of things put together that are related to the word "Meditation." People believe that meditation is just one thing, but what they do not realize is that meditation has a deeper view. There are many forms of meditation, and there are several ways to meditate. I'll give you my example of the time when I initially started meditating. I tried for the first few months and kept trying it for six to eight months. Eventually, I discovered that there was another approach, and so, I religiously followed that approach.

With the passage of time, I kept discovering new ways and followed them. I realized that there are a lot of trainings and methods available to practice meditation. There are a lot of people teaching it. Then I thought to ask the people teaching that how do they do it. I attended their training sessions and not to mention I paid a lot of money for that.

I attended different training sessions and learned different meditation techniques from different teachers. After learning all I could, I realized that there had to be something different. That is when I came up with "Quantum Mind Experience." I learned that there is a very specific way to take you from having a monkey mind to a quantum mind. However, before moving forward, it is important to understand the different types of meditations.

- **Mindfulness** – They are simple techniques to lower your brainwaves to deeply relax you. One of the exercises of mindfulness is the awareness of breathing. Our bodies have an internal function and an external function. The external function of our body is controlled by our minds. In other words, the mind helps the body move. However, the internal function of the body is not controlled by the mind. Breathing is the only thing that is not dependent on any other source, but rather it listens to the body too. Breathing is controlled by the human mind. However, it is run by the unconscious mind. Mindful meditation does nothing but relaxes you.
- **Visualization** – The second type of meditation is visualization. Visualization refers to imagination. It utilizes all of the human senses to see, smell, taste, hear, and feel. If you are part of the NLP world, then you would know that this meditation is performed quite a lot. People go to places visually and see things through their brains.
- **Healing** – A lot of people perform energy healing practice. Energy healing is a process where you sit quietly, and the other person in this healing process heals you with the help of chakras.

- **Intuitive** – Intuitive meditation helps in tapping into your intuition. It is known as hypnotherapy, psychedelic state, etc. It basically touches your unconscious mind when it is in the space before the mind goes to sleep.
- **Shadow** – It is used to heal your past memories. Regression Therapy is conducted in order to help you heal from your past. This type of meditation helps in healing ourselves in order to make yourself self-aware. Let's not forget that it gives us the ability to express ourselves in a more genuine manner.
- **Connection** – It is a specific way to establish and nurture a deeper connection between two or more people by tapping into higher levels of compassion. When we get into a relationship, we think about that person before going to bed. We build a connection with that person before even starting a relationship. Therefore, one can say that connection meditation is very effective if you are considering developing a relationship with that other individual.
- **Reprogramming** – This is an inner practice that is used to reprogram the past beliefs or breaking past behaviors that are no longer beneficial for you. A good example of this is NLP.
- **Quantum Mind** – Quantum mind practice is a transcendent practice into the future self, and it is all about building a new

character particle by particle. By transcendent practice, I mean, you need to get out of your old habits and character in order to build a new character. You basically transform yourself into a new person. This is how quantum mechanics work where you develop new things such as relations or habits just the way you want to create them. You have the chance to create that superhero of your life.

Simply put, the quantum practice goes from your analytical brain to your inner world attention brain, which is known as alpha brain waves. There are two types of brain waves; beta brain waves and alpha brain waves. These are the two types of different brain waves, and quantum practice helps in taking from one type to the other. The quantum world helps in creating changes in one's life. You can practice quantum meditation while walking, talking, sitting, sleeping, or doing anything else. There is an exact theory that is associated with the Quantum Mind.

Most people believe that we live in this world where all of us are linear beings living in a linear world. However, the truth is that we are dimensional beings living in a dimensional world. We all have a perception that we have come from somewhere, and we are going somewhere, but that is not how it is. Also, science has proved it. Each of us does not have problems understanding things intellectually.

For example, people are aware that they shouldn't be smoking. They know that junk food is not healthy. They are also aware of what their business needs, yet they do not cater to those needs. I was one of those people who knew what my business needed, yet I sat there, taking no action at all. With all these problems, if learning more was the answer, then there would be more billionaires than there are currently.

So how do we reach that next level? I truly believe that the Quantum Mind Experience is what will lead us to the next level. Here are some commercial types of meditation that are taught by others.

- **Transcendental Meditation (TNM)** – This type of meditation is based on mantras. You are given a mantra to work on. Its origin started with Maharishi Mahesh Yogi during the 1960s. He started the TNM, and a lot of people are still using it to this day.
- **Vipassana Meditation** – This type of meditation uses the same formula that is used by Buddha.
- **Kundalini Meditation** – Kundalini meditation was started in the same way, but in this type of meditation, you open up your chakra and have a certain kundalini way of doing it.
- **Zen Meditation** – Zen is more like the mindful meditation that watches your breathing.

- **Sound Meditation** – It is nothing more than working on some soundwaves where people play different sounds, and then meditation is done through those sound waves.

Quantum Mind Meditation

Quantum Mind is a daily mediation practice which you do it every day for at least 20-30 minutes to create your future identity. The way it works is that you consciously create your future identity and describe the attributes of that character first.

Each morning you tap into that character and feel the way this character would think, feel and act. In other words, you transcend yourself into future you every day!

THE FAST GROWTH METHOD

System

Chapter 21
How to Become an Authority to Your Niche Market *Fast*

"Nothing strengthens authority so much as silence."
— *Leonardo da Vinci*

Did you know that the Coaching and Consulting Market is set to reach $325 billion by the year 2025 from $107 billion in 2015, according to Forbes? The question here is, if this industry is going to reach $325 billion dollars, do you want to be a part of it?

If your answer is yes, then the one thing you need to learn is that, for things to change, you MUST change. I truly believe that the upcoming chapters are nothing more than just an initiation for you to change. It is nothing but a push for you to get started on this path. If you have been thinking to be on this path and are not aware of where to start, the next five chapters will help you on your path or if you have already been on this path for a while and don't know how to take your business to the next level, these chapters will assist in providing a system to scale your business.

You may find the information given in the next few chapters is repetitive and there is a reason for that. I want to make sure you understand the complete strategy and ready to apply. Also, if you like to revisit this book in the future just to cover the business aspects. You only have to read the last five chapters.

The Game Plan

When you are playing a game, no matter what game it is, you need to understand the semantics of that game. You need to understand the rules of the game you are playing. If you are trying to play soccer on a cricket pitch, you will most probably get kicked out. The reason being that every game has its own set of rules. In this game that we are playing, which is selling your skill set, no matter what the skill set, you need to understand the rule of this game. You need to understand what hat you are wearing when playing the game. For example, if you are playing soccer, then you need to understand if you are a goalie, a defender, or any other role. When you play a game, and you know what your role is, it becomes easier to play the game and be successful in it.

When playing cricket, you must know whether you are a batter or a baller, an opener or middle order. You need to know the level of the game that you are playing and what your role is going to be.

- **Coach** – In this industry, you can be a coach where you help other people attain certain goals. Certain people need your help because they do not know how to do it. In order to become a coach, you do not have to win a World Cup. You could simply be helping people win the World Cup by guiding them on how to play the game.

- **Mentor** – The person in this position is an expert in the relevant field, who passes on his experience to the newcomers. If you are a business person, you must have already made a business successful and have already learned the right and the wrongs. Now, you must be in a position where you are looking to help other people. You are called a mentor because you have already walked that path, and you are now showing other people how to walk on that path.
- **Consultant** – Consultants are the experts or advisors who help resolve a particular problem. Consultants are given very specific tasks to do.
- **Researcher** – These are the people who have obtained knowledge through extensive research, reading books, etc.
- **Authors** – These are those people who write on specific topics.
- **Trainer** – This person is an expert who teaches others the ins and outs of the game.
- **Connector** – As the name suggests, this person helps others connect. If you are part of multilevel marketing or any referral-based businesses, you are automatically a connector.

Your job is to connect point A to B. This is what multilevel marketing is about. It is not your job to manufacture items. However, your job is to connect the consumer to the manufacturer

Now the question here for you is, who are you in this game? What role are you playing? You may be playing more than one role. It is not necessary that you play only one role in your game. You can be a coach as well as an author as well as a trainer. It all depends on what you are willing to take up.

3-Step Process to Build Your Business

Most people provide a solution to fix a problem (band-aid). Someone may come running to you saying that his website is not working and so you offer a solution to fix their website. Some people may come saying they have a problem in their back, and they need a cure for it. You go ahead and fix their back. Some people may have a relationship issue, and you would provide them counseling regarding their relationship problems. That is where you are fixing the pain.

Most businesses today are doing the same. They are eradicating the pain of their clients. Therefore, if you are considering taking your business from $100,000 to $5 million, then you need to learn the following two steps. The second step is to educate them so they do not face those same problems in the future. Moreover, the third step is to influence them so they can join you on a journey to pleasure. If you run a business to fix the pain of the customers, you will end up making a very limited amount of money. After that, you need to educate your clients and then influence them to join you on a journey to pleasure. This is what will help take your business to the next level.

In the upcoming chapters, I will be covering the following topics:

- Step by Step process to help you become the authority of your target market
- Find out how to create an irresistible offer which your clients just can't say no to
- Learn how to create a presentation which sells
- Traffic, Leads and Conversion
- How to get 10-20 high-paying clients in the next 90 days using the fast growth system

How To Become an Authority of Your Niche Market *FAST*

If you want to have a consistent and predictable business, you need to be considered as a person of authority in your domain. In order to be an authority of a niche market, you need to know who your target market is. Also, in order to be an authority, you need to be very clear on the following three questions.

Who do you serve in your business?

What problem do you solve for your niche market?

What is your solution to their problem?

These questions need to be answered before you get into the content because if you don't, it becomes really hard for you to make a sale. Basically, these are clarity questions. These questions create clarity in your brain and in your clients' brains too. Without clarity, it just becomes really hard to sell. Once you have understood the above explanations, I will now move toward how to become a person with authority.

How to Become an Authority Fast?

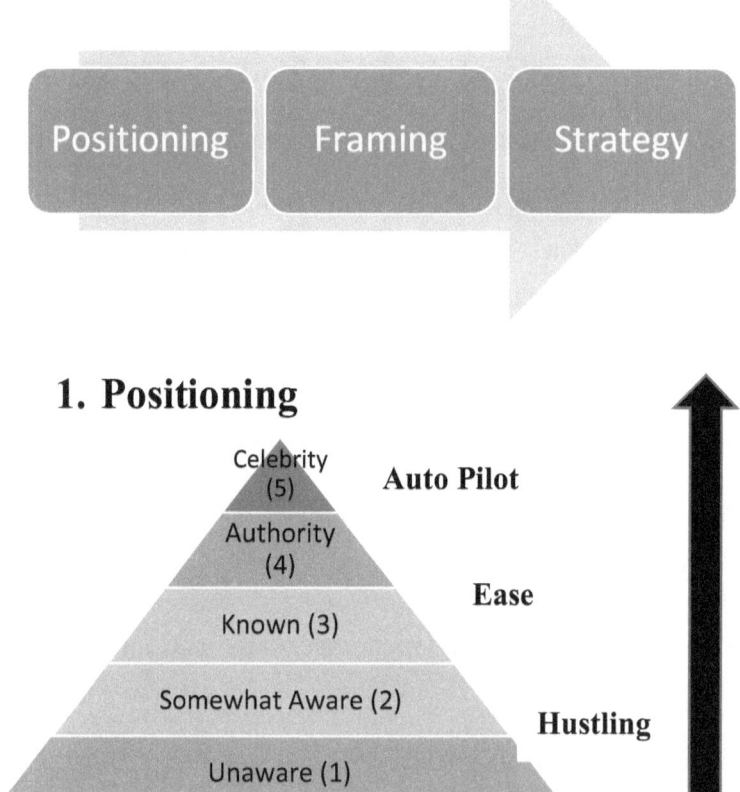

1. Positioning

THE FAST GROWTH METHOD

1. If your market is unaware of you and does not know about you, then you stand in the position to be hustling for clients. A lot of people may not have a clue about who you are and what you do.
2. In this phase, people know a little about you, but not that many people are aware of you.
3. This is where you are really known in the marketplace. When you are known for your business in your marketplace, business becomes easier for you as it becomes easy to get clients.
4. This is when you become an authority.
5. This is the stage when you become the celebrity of that domain you are in. When you become a celebrity, your business runs on autopilot. People come to you. You do not have to chase people or chase clients. They know you, and they come to you.

On the right-hand side of the image is an illustration of how you struggle to get your clients. If you are on the top, this means that your business is running on autopilot. Now the question is, where are you in this pyramid right now?

You probably know where you stand today. The next question you need to ask yourself is, where do you want to be?

A few things you need to keep in mind are that just because you made a decision today, it does not mean that it will come true. A decision has no meaning in itself unless you commit to it, and then you take massive action on it.

Here are the three steps you need to take to make it happen:

- Decide
- Commit
- Take Massive Action

You will get paid the most for your position in the marketplace. When your position is high, you will get paid the most. There are many people who make a good amount of money doing a job, whereas some people make millions doing a similar kind of job. It is all because of their positioning in the market. When you position yourself as an authority or as a celebrity of that domain, you can charge a high amount of money as well.

There are going to be many different businesses in the market, providing similar services or products as you do. It does not matter what sort of business you do; there are going to be a lot of other businesses. There are many people who are website developers, social media marketers, or any other experts. The question here is, if they all do the same thing, what is the one thing that separates them from each other? What is the superpower that separates you from the rest?

This is a statement that I use. You must use this statement too. Not in any marketing content, but just use it publicly like social media.

"[Your Name] is known as the most sought after [insert magic power or superhero identity] in the marketplace."

This statement is for you to use it to tell the world what you stand for. You do not have to be the best today; however, you will be what you claim you are with time.

Also, keep the end result in mind when designing statement like this. You must always talk about the results you can get for your clients. i.e. helping coaching reach 6-figure income

2. Framing

Framing is one of the important things that I have discovered, and I believe that it has changed my life and my business. Framing is used in marketing to control people's opinions and feelings about you and your brand. (not to be confused by NLP framing)

You know that in the marketplace, people are going to have a perception of you. Everybody sees and feels things differently. Wouldn't it be nice to be able to control those feelings? It would be great if you can do certain things and make sure you give them what to think about because it is a known fact that they are going to think about something regardless. They are going to create a perception anyways. It would be a great feeling to be able to control that.

Framing is a very specific content marketing strategy which controls the opinions and feelings of your potential client about you and your brand. So that people can know about you, like you, and trust you. When people start liking you and trusting you, they become willing to purchase from you.

The number one thing that prevents people from purchasing from you is the lack of trust.

3. Strategy

The content strategy that I am going to share with you works 100%. We have been using it for the past three years now. Not only in Australia but in other parts of the world too. This is what we created, which is also known as the Authority Content Quadrant™.

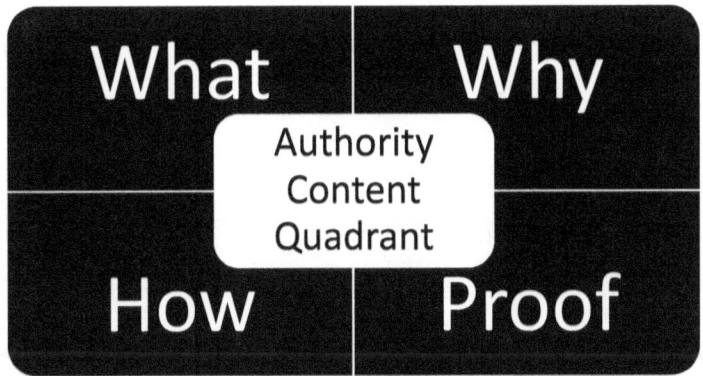

There is a special strategy behind creating content. It is not just anything randomly done. This quadrant is an engine, which runs and creates the content. This engine pretty much does most of the work. You have a "Why" type of content, a "What" content, a "How" content, and then you give social proof.

"Why" refers to why you do what you do. "What" refers to what you actually do. Then you talk about "How" you do it. What are the steps you take to solve people's problems? In the end, you show social proof. These proofs may be testimonials, success stories, etc.

Have you heard the saying, *"It's NOT what you know, It's WHO you know."* However, let me correct this sentence. *"It's NOT who you know. It's WHO knows YOU."* There are a few reasons as to why people just won't buy from you. They are:

- They do not have the desire to

- They don't trust you
- They don't see the value
- They don't find you credible

The entire reason for this strategy is to get people to know you, like you, and trust you. When you work with them, they already see you as an authority. Therefore, you do not need to use the concept of hard selling on them. After all, the reason for this strategy is to make your potential clients know you, like you, and trust you.

Here's a simple perception marketing strategy for you. There are few complex versions available as well but this will get you started on this path. We call it a 3x3 video strategy, as shown in the below image. This strategy is using Facebook sponsored ads to target your niche market.

You start with Why1 Video. If someone views your Why1 video for more than 50%, you send them to What1, but if they only watch Why1 for 10%, you send them to Why2 video. You do the same for What and How Videos. You only need to configure it one time. Once this engine starts to work, you can just change the audience or location to target a completely new market.

Remember what I said in the earlier chapters, sales is an elimination process. Most people will drop off and only few go through the entire Facebook Video funnel. Once they have gone

THE FAST GROWTH METHOD

through the entire funnel you offer them a FREE strategy session (more on this in chapter 25)

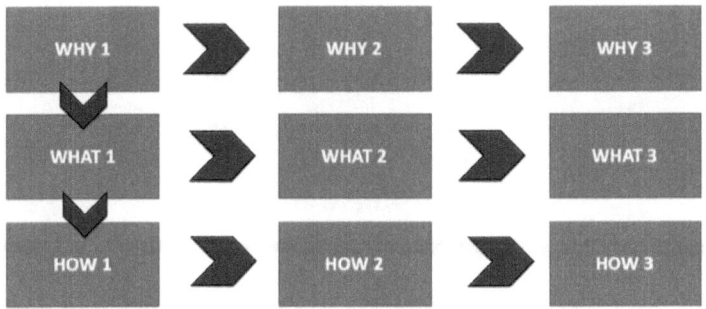

Chapter 22
Irresistible Product

"The people who are crazy enough to think they can change the world are the ones who do."

- *Steve Jobs*

This chapter is about Irresistible Products. This chapter has everything to do with how to create a product and give an offer to which your client just can't say NO to. A lot of people face problems in this topic, and with this chapter, I am going to demonstrate how to create a product that everybody wants.

The biggest problem that people come to us with is that they say that they do not have clients. They complain that they do not have enough leads. It is a big problem. But not having enough leads or clients is just a symptom of a bigger problem. It may seem like a big problem, but it is more of a symptom.

Let's look at how this gets started in our school system; we are taught that skills are the most important aspect of an individual. From day 1, we work hard on our skillset. You spend time learning all the different skills and enhancing them. The thing is that when you learn that skillset, you start to believe that skillset is more important. Let's say you spent five years in a university to learn a particular skill-set, i.e. accounting or information technology, then you take that skillset and go to the marketplace, and you apply for jobs that are relevant to your skills. The market refuses to hire you because it does not have a job for you. That's when you begin to curse the market. You start blaming the market that after spending five years in the university, studying and acquiring that skillset and now nobody has a job for you. You curse the market, and everything because of that.

Then, with time, you start to blame yourself. You begin with questions like, *"Am I lacking due to a language barrier?" "Am I lacking because I am not a local?"* You start pointing fingers toward yourself and find reasons for not getting a job. The reason may be that there is no job in the market. This is how the market works, and we start to believe that it is because we lack certain skillset. The third thing in the market is called The Product or Service. If you look at successful entrepreneurs as an example, they never look at themselves as a skillset.

They do not care about their skillset. All they care about is what is out in the marketplace, what is in demand, what's the problem, and whether or not they can fill the gap. They look at the market and determine which product or service can fill the gap. For example,

Richard Branson does not know how to fly a plane. He may know it now, but when he established the airline, he did not have a clue of how to fly a plane.

What he did is that he went and saw the marketplace, and he went to Boeing and planned on renting a plane. He hired the plane, took it to the marketplace, hired people to do the work, and today he is a successful man.

Have you ever wondered…you are so good at what you do, yet people do not buy from you? Why? Do you feel that you are the industry's best-kept secret? Nobody knows about you or about what you do.

It is not about how much you know, how much experience you have, what skill-set you possess. None of those things matter. The only thing that matters is whether your potential client **believes** that you have the ability to solve their problem. People are going to knock on your door only if they believe that you are capable of solving their problems. Let me give you an example of my life.

I was a person who failed in a lot of startups, and I didn't know why people were not buying from me. I remember going to a shopping center to see that people are buying from every shop in the center. I noticed that buyers were really happy when buying stuff. I then realized that people loved buying, but they don't like to be sold to.

After realizing this, I had to look back and search for a simple concept. I had to read a lot of books and attend a number of workshops to find the answer to this one fundamental question – why do people buy?

Why People Buy?

After conducting a lot of research to find the answer to this question, here is what I came up with. So everybody has their present reality where they are standing today. Everybody in the world, including you and me, have a desired future where we all want to get to. We all have a present reality and the desired future, and we all are buying things to go toward our desired future. So here is what you need to know. Your target market today also has a present reality where they are currently standing and are looking for certain results. They are also looking for a desired future, and there is a gap in between as well.

Your product is what will act as a prop through which you can fill that gap quicker and faster. As I have mentioned in the earlier chapters, the person or the company that fills that gap quicker and faster makes most of the money.

People do not buy your services; they buy the desired future.

Never Sell Vitamins in the Marketplace

There is an old saying in the marketing world that you never sell vitamins; you only sell painkillers. If you sell vitamins, it is a good-to-have product. When you sell good-to-have products, people are going to say they will think about buying it. If you want to build a business, you must learn how to cure the pain of others. There must be a certain pain in their mind, which you are fixing. If you don't do it and try to sell vitamins, then you are going to end up working really hard.

Let me make it a bit clear.

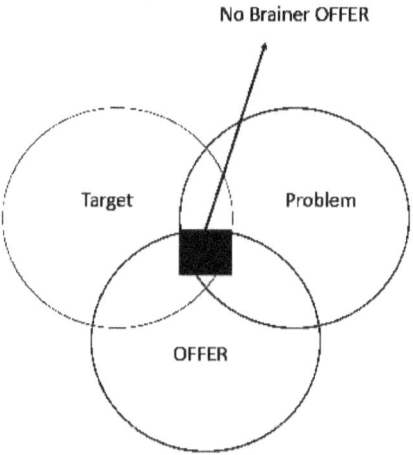

So there is a target market, the problem they have, and the offer that you provide to fix that problem. There is an area where all three things intersect. That area is the no brainer offer. Therefore, you do not have to serve the entire target market. If I say I want to work with IT professionals, it does not mean I will be working with all the IT professionals because they do not have the same problems, same beliefs and values.

One major mistake that most people make is that they try to solve every problem that their target markets have. They select a target market and choose to work with them for every problem they have. It is not a bad thing to solve every problem, but choosing one problem at a time makes things easier. When you take people to so many destinations, people become confused, and a confused client will never buy anything.

How to Deliver your Services?

You will find three types of people in the marketplace. One type is the people who want to learn and do things themselves. They will come to you to learn and do the rest by themselves. The other people will come to you asking for help for a certain period of time, and they will be on their own after that time. The third type of people are those who do not want to do anything themselves. Instead, they want things done for them. You will find these three types of people in any service-based business.

Nobody in the marketplace buys your products without any

awareness. They won't buy them because they do not care about your products or what you do. They only care whether or not you can help them get to their desired future. They are looking for some sort of vehicle that will get them to their desired future in a short period of time.

Problems People Have

As discussed earlier, there are three types of markets. Wealth market, Health market, and Relationship market. Everything within that is sub-market. Therefore, you need to understand the market you are operating in.

How to Find Out What People Want

A quick answer to the question regarding how to find out what people want is, ***just ask them***. Conduct market research and ask them what they really want. It is important that you do not end up creating a business based only on your assumptions. Assumptions usually turn out to be wrong, which can result in a major loss.

Any assumption that I come up with is based on my view of the world and the way I see things. Therefore, you need to make sure you ask the market and not assume the needs of your target market.

How You Can Help People?

These are the three things that you must have in your business.

- **Do-It-yourself:** You provide your market with online programs, eBooks, and online courses, and then you leave them to learn on their own.
- **Done With You:** You provide workshops, programs, and other similar things which run for a certain period of time. For example, a 3-day program, 5-day program, etc. You can also provide boot camps where people can come and work with you in a group setting.
- **1-on-1:** In this case, you help people 1-on-1. This is where you can charge a higher price depending on the industry you are operating in.

The way to expand any business is that you can take them to *one destination* by providing them different options to get there. The options above are the different options that you can offer to get there.

The below diagram is just an example of one destination. In the below example, you are taking people to Sydney from Melbourne and there are different options available to get them to the destination. So, remember this golden rule. Always taken them to one destination, once you get to Sydney, you can then take them to another destination.

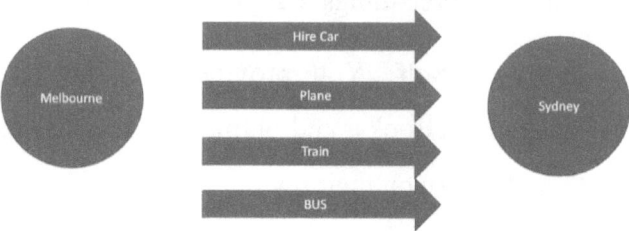

The big secret is that you provide them with the same information everywhere. The only difference is that some are high touch, and some of them are just online. Some of them may be more of you and less of them, whereas in some cases it may be more work for your clients and and less of you. That is the only difference.

More of you means more money and more time. Less of you means less money and less time.

3 Different Products with Different Pricing

How do I set the price of my products? If you are one of those who face troubles in pricing your products, I will provide you with a very general rule. If you are working on something online, the price is usually from $500 - $2000. If you are running a group, the prices are between $3000 - $8000 in Australia and in New Zealand. The pricing in the US and the UK is much different. If you are doing a 1-on-1, you can charge from $4000 - $30,000. Some people are charging 1-on-1 for $250 per session. This is a very different way of looking at it. This is the point where people do not value the 1-on-1 sessions. Therefore, you need to be in between the above-mentioned price range. If you do not set the price as per the standard, people perceive that you are not just as good as the rest of the market. If you want to be successful in this service-based business, you need to have an irresistible product. This irresistible product will act as a vehicle to take people to their desired future.

If you are looking to run a business that can function without you, then you need to have this irresistible product. Let me elaborate on how we do things in the Fast Growth Program. We conduct market research, a competition analysis, a product, and packaging. Most people make this mistake. Let's say you have a competitor in the market, who has been in the business for a while. Now, you come along, and you claim to provide the same services as your competitor. You eventually come to the realization that you have been specializing in a particular service since day 1, yet your competitor is way ahead of you. Your potential clients are aware of your competitor, and so, they prefer them over you.

The biggest mistake is that people do not look and start researching their competitors. They just establish a business because they believe that they are the only ones doing it. I suggest that you need to look at what your competitors are doing so that you can do it better in order to take over the market. In our Fast Growth Program, what we do is, we look at the competition and study what they are doing. Then, we do it in a better manner and provide a new opportunity for the target market. (not just an improvement offer). But for you to create a new opportunity for your target market, you must understand your competition really well. If you are already aware of how your competitor's product and services look like, you must add that difference on top of that so people can come to you instead of going elsewhere.

Do not start from the beginning, start from where their competition stops and add in 2mm on top of that. You could do small things such as improving support, improved service, or anything else. It is the little changes that matter the most. When you do that, your target market will notice you doing things better than the competition. Then you will see how your target market will change their direction from your competitor toward you.

Chapter 23
Present to Influence

"If they don't believe they can do it or can get results, they won't buy from you. Your presentation must build belief in your audience"

– Jag Jassel

If you are looking to influence people and would like people to:

- Move to take action
- Join your programs or community
- Buy your product / services

Then this is the chapter for you.

Before getting into the details, I want you to understand why it is so important to do this. When you work on the basis of 1-on-1 in your business, then, in that case, you most definitely have a client that you want to serve. When your business requires your time to run, it means that you are working as an employee in your own business.

This option is never going to grow your business to the next level. Why is that? Because we all have 24 hours. There is a limit where you can spend 1-on-1 with people. If you are working 1-to-many, then you have a business. In 1-to-many, you can have 50 people in the room. And if you are like Tony Robbins or Dalai Lama, you can even have 10,000 to 20,000 people in the room. It all depends on who you are and what you want to become. If you are starting and don't have many clients, then do not start with 1-to-many clients. If you already have 5-10 clients and you have done the work, then you can go ahead and do it.

What Do Most People do?

There are three variables to make more money. Time, rate, and client. If you want to make more money and increase your revenue, you can increase your rate your charge. Most people don't even look at any other variable, such as clients, and only look at the hours that you can charge and the time you spend at work.

The University system teaches us that the client variable is always constant. We never think about working on multiple jobs at the same time. During my early days, I always worked for one client. Even thought I was getting paid good amount on monthly basis but I always served one client. I had never thought that I could serve multiple clients simultaneously. Then I realized If I am doing the same thing, then why can't I do it with 5 different clients?

So, if you increase the number of clients, but you work the same number of hours, then what you get is double the amount. When you work 1-to-1, you focus on time. How do I know that the people I'm talking to have an employee mindset? They always talk about time. They always calculate how long it will take for them to complete the work. They always perceive the time variable to be the main variable.

When you work 1-to-many, you never charge based on the time. You charge based on the solution you are giving to them. The charges are never based on the hours, rather the solution to a problem. When working on 1-to-many, the focus is always on the solution because that is what the client is looking for. Employers look at the time you spent, whereas the clients look for the solution and how quickly you are able to find the solution. If you want to take your business to the next level, you need to learn how to serve 1-to-many. This is the one skill that will help you in growing your business. If you are making $100,000 today, you will be making a million dollars in no time. When you give a presentation, it should have the power to influence people to take action in a quick manner so their actions can take your business to the next level.

In the last 10 years, I have presented more than 1000 presentations. In 2017, when I sold my company, I started asking myself what I want to do now. Teaching is the first thing that came into mind. Despite past experience, runs on the board, nobody bought anything from me. Even though I had the money and credibility and worked for a lot of corporations, but no one made a purchase from me.

These two years of my life have been very interesting and challenging. However, it was very rewarding, as well. I have created 11 offers. In the last chapter, I explained about creating an irresistible offer. I have created 11 offers of my own. I sold via Evergreen Webinar, VSL, and Live Presentations.

My first 5 presentations were terrible, and I ended up selling nothing and earned nothing. I stood up, spoke, and shared my heart out in my presentations; however, I was making one big mistake. The reason I was not able to sell anything through my presentations because **I was teaching**. I stood up and taught.

*Therefore, the number one thing you should NEVER do is **teach**.*

When you teach them, your buyers stay in the friend-zone. They will come and shake your hands, appreciate what you say, thank you for your time but will never buy from you. Now the question is, what to do instead when you present?

You develop their **belief**. For example, if I give you the belief that you can do things the way I teach you, you will definitely buy the product. Like I have mentioned earlier, people don't buy for many reasons. One of them is that they do not have the desire to buy.

Another reason is that they do not trust you. The other factors are the credibility and value of the product. If you make their belief firm, then they will buy from you. Here, I want to teach you how to build their belief.

Your buyers need to believe in three things:

- Will I be able to do it?
- If I do it, will I be able to get the results?
- Are you the right person to show me the path?

If they believe in these three things, you can easily influence them. If they don't do it, you will struggle. Therefore, teaching is nowhere close to these events. Your presentation needs to follow a certain format to build that belief.

Here are the steps:

- Story
- Steps
- System

Story

How you achieved the desired results which your client is looking for.

In story, you show them how you did it. If you do not have a personal story, and you can't tell them how you did it, then show them what you have found in the marketplace. You can also show them by telling someone else's story and how they did it.

Go back to your life and create the steps on how you did it when you were in your clients' shoes. 80% of the people we work with are usually serving the kind of people who they were a few years ago, just like I am serving the same clients who I was before. I didn't know how to find clients, and I didn't know how to make my business successful. I kept failing again and again. Therefore, today I am serving the same people like me; they're just like how I was 5-6 years from now.

Steps

How to go from point A to point B. What are the steps?

In steps, you show them how they can do it. How they can get to their desired future. You give them the steps. You show them how people can do it themselves. At this point, you tell them the actual steps. The steps usually are 3, 5, or 7. And these steps become your recipe.

There are a lot of people out there who are doing the same thing as you are. They are serving the same clients as you are. They are solving a similar kind of problem. Your potential clients are looking for a system. So what you are doing is that by recipe, and by giving the system, you are telling them that you have steps and formula to follow. After that, you tell them your strategy as it is. My steps are known as the Fast Growth System, which comprises of 3 steps that will help you generate 20-30K a month. Those steps are the same strategy that I use for my business and for my high-paying clients.

System

What is your system (recipe) to get consistent results?

Show them how they can do it by using your system. At this point, you bundle the steps together and show them as a system how you can help them in the next 90 days or the next 30 days. A system provides a predictable and consistent outcome. McDonald's has a system. In the same way, IBM has a system. Even Tony Robbin's research company has a system.

The main thing to remember is that your presentation must create a gap. If your presentation fails to create a gap, they won't buy it. The gap is the difference between where they are today and where they want to go. If they do not feel that there is a gap, they will not buy. In the end, you need to show them how your system can fill the gap for them.

How You Can "Present" your Presentation?

- Live Events
- Online Master Classes / Webinars
- Video Sales Letter (VSL)

Once a presentation works, you keep it as it is. You do not change anything. Amateurs change presentations every week, but a professional maintains the same presentation because it works every time. Once it works, you execute it everywhere. If they like your presentation, they will like you too. Whereas, if they believe in your presentation, then they will definitely buy from you.

Chapter 24
Traffic, Leads & Conversion

"You must measure attention, leads and conversion on daily basis in your business"

– Jag Jassel

Melbourne's Lygon Street is very famous for Italian food. It is a food place where you can walk into any restaurant, and you will definitely get some good food. Now imagine your business being on that street. Look from an external perspective. Your client will walk onto that street and would be confused because of so many options since everything would look pretty much the same.

Now let me introduce you to Marco Donnini. He owns one of the oldest restaurants on Lygon Street. His family has been running the restaurant since 1982. They were the first ones who had installed the Espresso machine in their restaurant. Nonetheless, they faced problems such as there were too many options on the street, and there was not much foot traffic on Lygon Street. People would walk onto Lygon Street only to eat. Otherwise, no one really walked on that street.

Today, the same restaurant is one of the busiest places on Lygon

Street, where you cannot find a seat. They have won many awards and now have millions of dollars of turnover in their restaurant. Let's see how that happened in this chapter.

3 Key Metrics to Grow Any Business

Ask the following questions:

- How much attention are you getting?
- How many leads are you getting?
- What is the conversion rate on those leads?

5 Big Mistakes That Everyone is Making

1. Product is everything – Most people believe that their product or service is everything. They spend all their time to make their product the best in the world.

2. No Focus on Marketing & Sales

3. No <u>Authority</u>

4. No Lead Automation

5. No Measurement

Your biggest resource is time. So, you establish a business, you spend all your time on operational stuff, and after some time when you don't get any client for your business you are ready to close the business. Therefore, you develop this belief that the business is too hard and it is not for you. You blame the market for not helping you. You start blaming your sales team, your development team or your manufacturing team for your failures. You shut down your business, and you build this belief that doing business is the worst decision you have ever made.

If you know what to measure, then can you improve and measure it, right? Let me explain what you should measure in your business today.

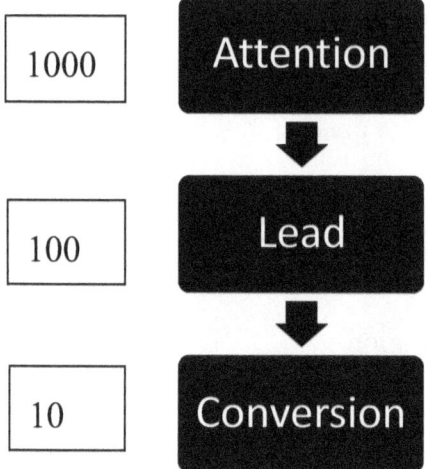

Business is a linear and sequential process. If you keep telling yourself that you don't have clients, my question would be to go back last month and calculate how much attention you got. How many leads did you get? How many conversions were you able to do? If you haven't done anything, then that means that you have a problem with attention (to begin with), then leads, and conversion. Not having clients is just a symptom. The big problem is this matrix. No attention, hence, no leads and no conversion. In the above example: To make 10 sales, you must have attention of 1000 people.

Now, you can pinpoint where is the exact problem.

Everything starts with attention.

It is important to see that when you do not have a client, you do not have a business. And when you do not have clients, all your focus should shift toward attention, lead, and conversion.

How to Create a FLOW in Your Business?

As a business owner, the number one thing that we all are seeking is attention. Attention of our prospects. If you are not getting attention from your prospects, you have a *message to market* problem. It means that whatever you are selling, your clients are not interested in buying it. Therefore, all your hypotheses about the problem might be wrong.

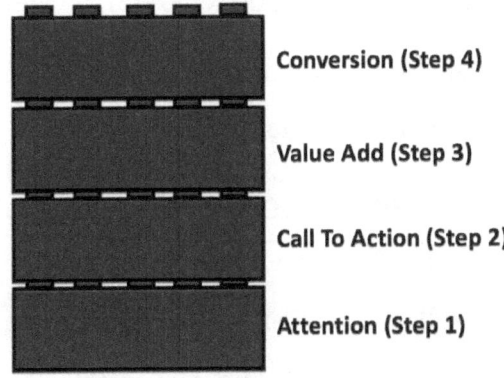

The reason it is called a hypothesis is that it is in your mind. It hasn't been proven. And if it is not proven, then it means that the client hasn't paid for it. It is just in your mind when you assume that there is a problem, but the client has not paid you for that. Until the client pays you, the problems are nothing but assumptions. Therefore, *attention* is important in order to bring flow to your business. If you are not getting it, then you need to go back and read chapter 13 again.

The question you must be asking yourself is, how do I get attention of my niche market?

Secondly, you need to have some kind of call to action. Whatever the action may be, you must make them take action. You need to make them either download your eBook, attend your workshop or webinar, join your group, etc. Without action, you can never know if your client is becoming a lead or not. The only way you can convert attention to lead is by some sort of call to action.

After that, you add value. You give your prospects what they are seeking. Then you move toward conversions.

How to Become the Go-To Person?

You probably know now that if you want to have your business run on auto-pilot, you must be considered as a go-to person of your niche market. If you recall, we have talked about this earlier that in any given time, only 10% people are ready to buy. They are in the market looking for solution. 80% of are not yet in the market to buy. You must have a strategy which target those 80% of your target market those are not yet ready to buy.

A perfect strategy is to provide high quality content to those 80% market. So now the question is, how to provide high quality content? Here's some examples, you can teach them something, interview them, motivate them, inspire them, and provide them case study examples, or even do Q&As to provide them with high-quality content.

This content must be specifically for your target market and not for you. Try to look at things from a client's perspective. In this stage, when you know you want to teach, inspire, and motivate them, you plant a high-quality seed. How do you do that?

You can do that through a book, an eBook, an online event, a 3-day or 5-day challenge, or a LIVE event, Facebook Live, Webinar etc.

There are two things that you can do. You can either go out and find where they are, or you can bring them to your room and plant a seed. (I find the later strategy works the best)

Your content strategy must target 5 types of clients.

- **Unaware** – These are people who do not have an idea of the problem they have. They have no clue that they are facing a problem. For example: I play hockey every day but have no problems yet.
- **Problem Aware** – These are the people who are aware of the problem. Example: One day while playing hockey, I injured my back. Now I am problem aware

- **Solution Aware** – These people know that they have a problem, and they are aware of the relevant solutions that are available in the market. After I injured my back, now I am aware that there are few solutions available in the marketplace that can help me cure my back problem i.e. remedial massage, doctor, Acupuncture, GP etc.
- **Product Aware** – These are those people who have searched the market and have come up with products that will help them solve the problem they are facing. Now I have researched the market and decided to go with remedial massage.
- **Most Aware** – These people are ready to make a decision to select the best product that will help them in solving their problem. Now I am looking for a remedial massage solution provider in my area.

The question you need to be asking is Who, Where, and What?

- Who are they?
- Where are they?
- What seed do I need to plant?

If you are a business coach and you are looking to expand your business, you need to focus on who the people are that you want to speak to. Where are these people located? And what seed do you need to plant?

The key here is Farming. Not chasing, not hunting, and not running after your clients. ***The secret is Farming.***

What is the Best Seed that Will Work in Any Industry?

Now you know that you have a seed of service. You have a seed that you are looking to deliver to your client. How would you give it to them? You do it through Webinars, Workshops and events. This is the best way to plant a seed.

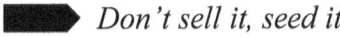 *Don't sell it, seed it*

How Can You Reach More People?

The answer to this question is, ***Go Through People and Not to People***. If you go to people individually, it is going to take a lot of time. Therefore, it is better to go through people instead of going to people. This way you can see and meet a lot of people.

Let us go back to Marco. What did he do? He spent his time building partnerships. He built partnerships with offices, hotels, Melbourne City Council, Carlton Footy Club, and many other partnerships.

Before you start thinking about developing joint venture

partnerships, you must be aware of the following three questions. These are the questions you JV partner have in his/her mind. These are the three questions that your partner is going to thinking about before he/she says yes to you.

- Do I trust him/her?
- Will he/she make me money?
- Will he/she make me look good?

If the answer to all these questions is YES, then they will be happy to be partners with you. Therefore, before you go and speak to somebody and ask to form a partnership, you need to answer these questions.

Let's look at the Fast Growth System now!

Chapter 25
The Fast Growth System

"With a business system operating in nearly 200 countries, we are not immune to the economic difficulties that currently exist in many markets around the world"

– M.Douglas Invester

In this chapter, I will share our complete system. This is the ONE system that is responsible for adding million in our client's businesses. If you follow this system step by step, I have no doubt that you will be able to grow your business ***FAST***.

Did you know that the coaching & consultation industry is the second-fastest growing industry today? According to Forbes, it is a $1 billion industry in the US alone, and it is growing by each day. So, if it is a $1 billion industry, then are you enjoying your share of that success? Are the perfect clients knocking at your door every day? Or do you wake up every morning not knowing where the next client is going to come from? If you have answered yes to the last question, then this system is for you. The Fast Growth System is designed for a very specific reason. It is designed to create a predictable business.

My mission is that I want to help coaches, consultants, and professional service providers to create a freedom business, serve millions, and make millions. But the sad truth about coaching and consulting industry is that anyone can call themselves a coach or a consultant, and that's how clients don't know who to trust. There are many so called guru's in the marketplace. Most service providers charge on an hourly rate, which is why 90% of them make less than $70,000 annually. They work mainly on 1-on-1, which means that they are trading time for money. They work 50+ hours a week, which is worse than a job. My goal for this last chapter is to share our complete system with you, and I want to demonstrate how you can get 10-20 high-paying clients in the next 90 days. I will share the exact same recipe that I used in my business, and because of that, we have hundreds of clients paying thousands of dollars to implement the same recipe.

Let's me share my journey again, you may recall three phases of my life that have made a huge difference in my life. The first phase was in 2010 when my son was born. At that time, I was working for a company called Oracle, and I was getting paid a really good amount of money. I was earning high six figures at that time, but then I started ask myself that there is more to life than this 9 to 5 job. Before that, It never occurred to me that I could make money just by running a business. I always thought that the only way to make money would be by working for somebody else. At that time, I started looking for different business opportunities, and the next five years became a huge struggle. I tried many things, but nothing seemed to work. I started to look for many business opportunities. I joined Multi-Level Marketing, opened up many consulting companies. Overall, I *failed, failed, and failed.*

The next five years for me were full of trial and error. I failed in 13 startups and lost more than $200,000+ in different business ventures. In the year 2015, I went to see the BIG guy, Mr. Tony Robbins, for the first time. I still remember he said this one thing, which made a huge difference in my life.

He said: *"Find someone who has already done what you are trying to do and ask for help."*

What I am going to share with you is a system. If you model the exact system, you will get the same results as many of our other students.

"The definition of insanity is doing the same thing over and over again, but expecting different results." Most people keep doing the same thing, again and again, every month and then they complain why they are not getting the results.

Here's what you need to be successful in your business today.

- A perfect marketing SYSTEM, which will capture the attention of your audience and generate unlimited quality leads.
- You MUST know how to get your prospects to know you, like you, and trust you in less than 24 hours and make them desperate to talk to you.
- I will share a simple conversion model which takes warm leads to high-paying clients.

Just keep in mind that I have shared some of the above in detail in the earlier chapters. This chapter is to show you how to put different pieces together and create a system which is replicable for you and your clients.

Let me ask you a question. What is the difference between McDonald's and a local burger joint? What is the difference between KFC and a local fried chicken shop? What is the difference between local IT consulting and IBM? And what is the difference between Tony Robbins Research Company and you?

The difference is the *SYSTEM*.

THE FAST GROWTH METHOD

What is the system? A system means to put certain input in it and get a predictable output on the other side. A good example would be when you walk into McDonald's, and it does not matter what you purchase or where you purchase it from. McDonald's tastes the same everywhere. The same theory applies to Tony Robbins. It doesn't matter where you attend his program; they provide the same experience. That is mainly because they use a ***system***.

The five big mistakes that most people are making today.

- Doing it alone,
- Not following a system,
- Selling to everyone,
- Doing trial and error,
- Trying to figure out everything by themselves without having any experience.

The answer is the fast growth system

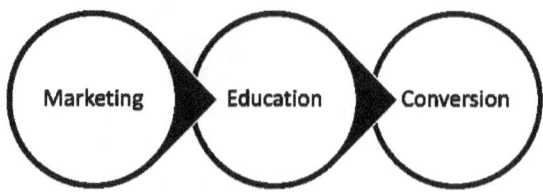

The way to avoid these mistakes is to follow a 3-step Fast Growth System.

- You need to have a marketing system that generates quality leads. In that case, you do not have to worry about where the next client is going to come from.
- You must educate your potential clients by teaching them how you can solve their problems.
- Also, you need to implement a conversion process, which is not a selling process, and it is designed to help people and not sell your programs.

Let's look at each of them in detail:

Secret 1: Marketing System – How to Capture the Attention of your Audience and Generate Quality Leads

There are three requirements of a perfect marketing system:

- Grab attention
- Make people agitated

- Take action

Before I discovered the three steps I was posting a lot of social media content, podcasts, had a YouTube channel, would do Facebook live videos, have Facebook groups, Twitter, LinkedIn, Instagram, blogs, vlogs; I was basically a social butterfly where I would attend all kinds of meetings, events, and business lunches thinking that this is how I would get clients. I had a huge fear of missing out (FOMO). Therefore, I was spending so much time doing all that, but I did not have time for my business. I was frustrated, and I was not getting any results or money in my bank. This was when I discovered this marketing system.

What should you be doing? You should be setting up Facebook ads. Why Facebook ads? The answer is because there are 2 billion people present on one platform. It is the best marketing product today with 15 million+ users in Australia alone. The Facebook algorithm knows more about you and your clients.

How to Make Facebook Ads Work For You?
- Stop trying to be creative and do what works the best.
- Don't stand out; try to go with the flow.
- Focus on the Problem and the Emotion your target market are feeling.

- Don't do 100 things; just do ONE thing right.
- Most importantly, check out your competitors Ads www.facebook.com/ads/library

The objective of Facebook ads is to make people "Click" the link. The objective is not to make people buy. Rather, it is to make people click. To do that you need for your perfect Facebook Ad copy:

- A single image
- Post a long Facebook ad with your story, your Aha moment, who is it for, and what problem can you help solve. Make sure to include all of these materials in the ad copy.

One thing to keep in mind is that **organic is slow, whereas paid is fast**. If you spend $1000-$3000 a month, you will be able to produce $3000 to $20,000 per month.

Step 1 of the system is Facebook Ads

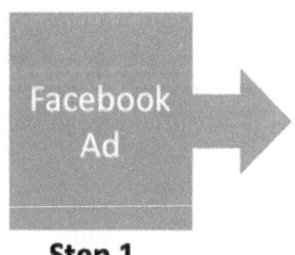

Step 1

Secret 2: How to Take your Prospect to Know You, Like You and Trust You in Less Than 24 Hours?

"If people like you, they will listen to you. But if they TRUST you, they will do business with you." - Zig Ziglar

So how can you make people like you and trust you in a short period of time? The answer is, *educate them*. Our brain is wired in a way to trick us into trusting people who educate us. Now the question is, "Most people educate, but why do people still not make the purchase?"

Education has 3 steps that you must follow in sequence:

- Build a belief in them
- Teach them
- Support them

Step 1: When you speak to sell, you must develop belief within your audience. If there is no belief, then expect there will be no sales. If your prospects don't believe that they can do it too or they can get the results they want, then they will not buy from you.

Step 2: After they have paid you, you now teach them. If there is no pay, there is no gain. Golden rule, you never teach until they have paid you because they haven't invested in you or your program. I have shared my $4000 program with my friends and family for FREE and none of them did anything with it. They simply didn't take any action. So people who pay, pay attention.

Step 3: Once you have taught them, you must support them. If there is no action, there are no results. You need to keep in mind that people sometimes get lazy; therefore, they need to be supported on their journey. If they don't take action, they won't get results and you won't get testimonials.

How You Can Teach Them?

As covered mostly in the chapter, "Present To Influence," You can record a video presentation of about 25 to 45 minutes. During this presentation, you teach them about certain problems and emotions. Most people talk about problems, but they forget to talk about the emotions they feel when facing such problems. Therefore, it is important that you talk about their emotions too.

To get people to move and take action, they must feel four emotions, i.e. hope, trust, excitement, and urgency. The objective of the presentation is to urge people to book a phone call with you.

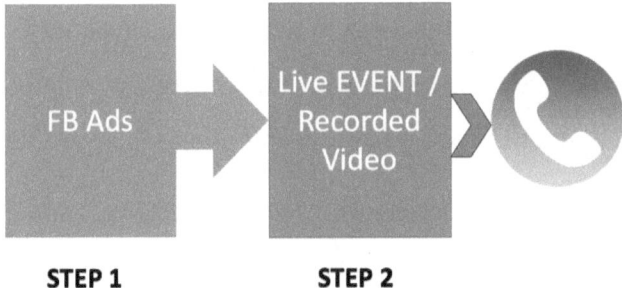

STEP 1   **STEP 2**

Secret 3: A Simple Conversion Model Which Takes Warm Leads to High Paying Clients

The conversion process is a process that converts a stranger into a high-paying client. As discussed in the chapter 15, your only job on the call is to make a ***diagnosis***. You need to conduct a diagnosis just like how a doctor diagnoses the patient.

One of the biggest mistakes I have seen people making is that they start to coach, consultant or try to provide solutions on these sales calls. When you are on a call, you must NOT coach them, consult them or try to solve their problem by providing them with solutions.

When people tell you the problem on the call, you can just say, "Ok." Once again, don't try to solve their problem until they become a paying client.

Find out their current situation, desired future and the gap. Once you have a clear understanding of the gap, place your product / services as a vehicle for them to achieve their desired future. Most people make the mistake of selling their program or product on the call. What you need to do is sell a solution to their problem.

Here is a 9-step conversion process to convert on a call. If you use the following system, I can promise you that you will get anyone enrolled in buying your product or services.

1. Chat for 2 minutes
2. Set the agenda
3. Find where they are at in the current situation
4. What is the problem?
5. Find out their desired future
6. Find out why they want the desired future
7. Acknowledge the gap
8. Who you are, and what do you do?
9. State your offer and explain how it works

After you state your offer and your package, your prospects will ask you the price. Do not mention the price of your product until asked. Once you quote the price, then you must shut-up and wait for the response. The silence may be of one to two minutes sometimes but do not try to fill this silence with anything. It will be very awkward in the beginning but after some calls you will get used to it. Once again, don't try to fill this silence with anything. The first person to speak will be at a loss.

The next step would be to get them started.

The magic formula is;

Diagnosis Call = Sale!

The Fast Growth System

In the end, I would like to say one thing. ***Be consistent.*** You won't see the results straight away but trust the process and be consistent on the path.

Now I want to invite you to hang out with me and other amazing people in my world. Spend time in our Facebook Group, watch our videos, and make friends with other people like you. With that said, I encourage you to master the system and method mentioned in this book.

Thank you for spending this time with me.

To Your Success!

Jag Jassel

THE FAST GROWTH METHOD

Very special thanks to Tony Robbins, Sir Richard Branson, Dr. Wayne Dyer, Russell Brunson, Brendon Burchard, Ray Dalio, Dr. Deepak Chopra, Christopher Duncan, Sam Ovens, Vishen Lakhiani, and Frank Kern!

www.ingramcontent.com/pod-product-compliance
Lightning Source LLC
Chambersburg PA
CBHW030608220526
45463CB00004B/1215